D0542883

Islâm: Its Foundations and Concepts

First Edition: August 2006

Supervised by:
ABDUL MALIK MUJAHID

© **Maktaba Dar-us-Salam, 2006**
King Fahd National Library Cataloging-in-Publication Data
As-Suhaym, Muhammad bin Abdullah
    Islam: Its foundations and concepts/Muhammad bin
    Abdullah As-Suhaym - Riyadh, 2006
    238p ; 21cm
ISBN: 9960-9801-6-2
    1- Is,am 2- Islam - General principles
    I- Title
    210 dc   1427/4201
    L.D. no. 1427/4201
    ISBN: 9960-9801-6-2

Islâm: Its Foundations and Concepts

By: Dr. Muhammad bin Abdullaah As-Suhaym

Translated by

Abdur-Raafi Adewale Imâm
Under The Supervision of
Translation and Publication Division,
Islâmic Propagation And Education Committee,
Muslim World League
Al-Madinah Al-Munawwarah
Tel. 8150133, 8150144

DARUSSALAM
GLOBAL LEADER IN ISLAMIC BOOKS
Riyadh, Jeddah, Sharjah, Lahore
London, Houston, New York

HEAD OFFICE

P.O. Box: 22743, Riyadh 11416 K.S.A.Tel: 0096 -1-4033962/4043432 Fax: 4021659
E-mail:darussalam@awalnet.net.sa, riyadh@dar-us-salam.com, Website: www.dar-us-salam.com

K.S.A. Darussalam Showrooms:
- **Riyadh**
Olaya branch: Tel 00966-1-4614483 Fax: 4644945
Malaz branch: Tel 00966-1-4735220 Fax: 4735221
- **Jeddah**
  Tel: 00966-2-6879254 Fax: 6336270
- **Madinah**
  Tel: 00966-503417155 Fax: 04-8151121
- **Al-Khobar**
  Tel: 00966-3-8692900 Fax: 8691551
- **Khamis Mushayt**
  Tel & Fax: 00966-072207055

U.A.E
- **Darussalam, Sharjah U.A.E**
  Tel: 00971-6-5632623 Fax: 5632624
  Sharjah@dar-us-salam.com.

PAKISTAN
- **Darussalam, 36 B Lower Mall, Lahore**
  Tel: 0092-42-724 0024 Fax: 7354072
- **Rahman Market, Ghazni Street,**Urdu Bazar Lahore
  Tel: 0092-42-7120054 Fax: 7320703
- **Karachi,** Tel: 0092-21-4393936 Fax: 4393937
- **Islamabad,** Tel: 0092-51-2500237

U.S.A
- **Darussalam, Houston**
  P.O Box: 79194 Tx 77279
  Tel: 001-713-722 0419 Fax: 001-713-722 0431
  E-mail: houston@dar-us-salam.com
- **Darussalam, New York** 481 Atlantic Ave, Brooklyn
  New York-11217, Tel: 001-718-625 5925
  Fax: 718-625 1511
  E-mail: newyork@dar-us-salam.com.

U.K
- **Darussalam International Publications Ltd.**
  Leyton Business Centre
  Unit-17, Etloe Road, Leyton, London, E10 7BT
  Tel: 0044 20 8539 4885 Fax:0044 20 8539 4889
  Website: www.darussalam.com
  Email: info@darussalam.com
- **Darussalam International Publications Limited**
  Regents Park Mosque, 146 Park Road
  London NW8 7RG Tel: 0044- 207 725 2246

AUSTRALIA
- **Darussalam** 153, Haldon St, Lakemba (Sydney)
  NSW 2195, Australia
  Tel: 0061-2-97407188 Fax: 0061-2-97407199
  Mobile: 0061-414580813 Res: 0061-2-97580190
  Email: abumuaaz@hotamail.com

CANADA
- Islmic Books Service
  2200 South Sheridan way Mississauga,
  Ontario Canada L5K 2C8
  Tel:001-905-403-8406 Ext. 218 Fax: 905-8409

HONG KONG
- **Peacetech**
  A2, 4/F Tsim Sha Mansion
  83-87 Nathan Road Tsimbatsui
  Kowloon, Hong Kong
  Tel: 00852 2369 2722 Fax: 00852-23692944
  Mobile: 00852 97123624

MALAYSIA
- **Darussalam International Publication Ltd.**
  No.109A, Jalan SS 21/1A, Damansara Utama,
  47400, Petaling Jaya, Selangor, Darul Ehsan, Malaysia
  Tel: 00603 7710 9750 Fax: 7710 0749
  E-mail: darussalm@streamyx.com

FRANCE
- **Editions & Librairie Essalam**
  135, Bd de Ménilmontant- 75011 Paris
  Tél: 0033-01- 43 38 19 56/ 44 83
  Fax:0033-01-43 57 44 31 E-mail: essalam@essalam.com.

SINGAPORE
- Muslim Converts Association of Singapore
  32 Onan Road The Galaxy
  Singapore- 424484
  Tel: 0065-440 6924, 348 8344 Fax: 440 6724

SRI LANKA
- Darul Kitab 6, Nimal Road, Colombo-4
  Tel: 0094 115 358712 Fax: 115-358713

INDIA
- Islamic Books International Mumbai-India
  54 Tandel Street (North)
  Dongri, Mumbai 4000 009,India
  Tel: 0091-22-2373 68 75, Fax:2373 0689
  E-mail:sales@irf.net

SOUTH AFRICA
- Islamic Da'wah Movement (IDM)
  48009 Qualbert 4078 Durban,South Africa
  Tel: 0027-31-304-6883 Fax: 0027-31-305-1292
  E-mail: ldm@ion.co.za

CONTENTS

Translator's Note 7

Author's Preface 9

Where is the Way? 15

Existence of Allah, His Lordship 16

One: Creation of Universe and Its
Wonderful Design 21

Two: The Nature 22

Three: Consensus of All People 24

Four: The Reason 25

Creation of the Universe 35

The Underlying Reasons 40

Creating and Honouring Man 47

Why Was Man Created? 59

Man's Need for Religion 63

General Criteria of the True Religion 69

Types of Religions 78

Conditions of the Existing Religions 83

The Essence of Prophethood 93

Signs of Prophethood 101

Mankind's Need for the Messengers 105

The Final Return 113

Fundamentals of the Messenger's Mission   121

The Everlasting Message   127

The Seal of Prophethood   139

The Meaning of the Word: Islam   143

  Definition of Islâm   143

  The Reality of Islâm   144

  Reality of Disbelief   147

Sources of Islâm   153

  A. The Glorious Qur'an: 153

The First Degree   167

The Second Degree   177

  One: Belief in Allâh.   177

  Two: Benefits of Belief in Angels   180

  Three: Belief in the Books   182

  Four: Belief in the Messengers   186

  Five: Belief in the Last Day   190

  Six: Belief in Pre-decree   195

The Third Degree   201

Some Beauties of Islam   205

Repentance   215

The End of One Who Does Not Adhere to Islam   221

The End   235

Translator's Note

In the name of Allah, Most Gracious, Most Merciful

All praise is due to Allah. May peace and blessings be upon the Messenger ﷺ, his household and Companions.

This book is undoubtedly a commendable attempt at showing the beauties of Islam to mankind, drawing a comparison between this great religion and other world religions in spiritual, moral, social and intellectual aspects and acquainting mankind with its principles and fundamentals in a logical, unambiguous, convincing frank but gracious manner.

We would however like to call the attention of the reader to some points as regards the translation of some of the quotes and foreign names in this book. The author quoted some passages from the Bible and other books which are not originally Arabic. Though we believe that the proper academic method in translating these passages is to refer to their original sources since most of them are in English, we could not however do so because of their unavailability to the translator. It is therefore hoped that, translation of the passages rendered here are as close as possible in meaning, to the original texts.

As for the names of some authors mentioned in the Book in Arabic letters, we exerted efforts to know the correct spelling of these names in their original languages. But due to the fact that the author quoted excerpts from their books from secondary sources which are in Arabic, we could not have access to the original books; hence the names were transliterated from Arabic.

Equally, the names of foreign references mentioned in this book in English may not be the exact names given by their various authors. Most of these are translated from Arabic.

May Allah make this book beneficial for all and reward its author abundantly in this world and the Hereafter.

Abdur-Raafi Adewale Imâm

Author's Preface

All praise is due to Allâh. We praise Him, seek for His assistance and forgiveness and we seek refuge with Him from evils of our souls and our misdeeds. No one can mislead whosoever Allâh guides and none can guide whosoever Allâh causes to go astray.

I testify that there is no deity worthy of worship except Allâh alone. He has no partner. I also testify that Muhammad ﷺ is His slave and Messenger.

Allâh sent Messengers to mankind in order that people may not have any plea against Him after He has sent these Messengers. He also revealed Books as guidance, mercy, light and healing.

In the past, Messengers were especially sent to their people and entrusted with the preservation of their book. That was why their writings became forgotten and their laws became altered, because they were sent to a specific nation on a limited period.

Thereafter, Allâh chose His Prophet Muhammad ﷺ and made him the last of all Prophets and Messengers. He says,

﴿مَّا كَانَ مُحَمَّدٌ أَبَآ أَحَدٍ مِّن رِّجَالِكُمْ وَلَٰكِن رَّسُولَ ٱللَّهِ وَخَاتَمَ ٱلنَّبِيِّـۧنَ﴾

"Muhammad is not the father of anyone among you, but he is the Messenger of Allâh and the last (end) of the Prophets." [1]

---

[1] (Al-Ahzâb 33:40)

Allâh honoured him with the best Revealed Book which is the glorious Qur'ân; He took it upon Himself to preserve it and did not assign the obligation of its preservation to any of His creatures. He says:

﴿إِنَّا نَحْنُ نَزَّلْنَا ٱلذِّكْرَ وَإِنَّا لَهُۥ لَحَٰفِظُونَ﴾

"Verily, We it is Who have sent down the Dhikr (i.e., Qur'ân) and surely, We will guard it (from corruption)." [1]

He also makes the Law of Muhammad the lasting one till the Day of Resurrection. He explained that the perpetuity of his Law necessitates the belief in it, calling unto it and being patient with it. Hence the path of the Prophet ﷺ and his followers is that of calling to the way of Allâh with sure knowledge. While making this *manhaj* clear, Allâh says:

﴿قُلْ هَٰذِهِۦ سَبِيلِىٓ أَدْعُوٓاْ إِلَى ٱللَّهِ عَلَىٰ بَصِيرَةٍ أَنَا۠ وَمَنِ ٱتَّبَعَنِى وَسُبْحَٰنَ ٱللَّهِ وَمَآ أَنَا۠ مِنَ ٱلْمُشْرِكِينَ﴾

"Say (O Muhammad): This is my way; I invite unto Allâh with sure knowledge, I and whosoever follows me. And Glorified and Exalted be Allâh. And I am not of the polytheists." [2]

Allâh commanded the Prophet to bear whatever harm he suffered in the cause of Allâh with patience and says:

﴿فَٱصْبِرْ كَمَا صَبَرَ أُوْلُواْ ٱلْعَزْمِ مِنَ ٱلرُّسُلِ﴾

---

[1] Al-Hijr 15:9
[2] Yûsuf 12:108

"Therefore be patient (O Muhammad ﷺ) as did the Messengers of strong will." [1]

He also enjoins patience on Muslims,

﴿يَـٰٓأَيُّهَا ٱلَّذِينَ ءَامَنُوا۟ ٱصْبِرُوا۟ وَصَابِرُوا۟ وَرَابِطُوا۟ وَٱتَّقُوا۟ ٱللَّهَ لَعَلَّكُمْ تُفْلِحُونَ﴾

"O you who believe! Endure and be more patient and guard (your territory by stationing army units permanently at the places from where the enemy can attack you) and fear Allâh, so that you may be successful." [2]

In accordance with this gracious Divine Way, I write this book to invite people to the religion of Allâh, deriving guidance in doing so, from the Book of Allâh and the *Sunnah* of His Messenger ﷺ. I briefly explained herein the story of the creation of the Universe, the creation of man and how he was favoured by sending Messengers to him and situation of past religions. I afterwards made an introduction to Islâm as per its meaning and pillars. So, whoever is looking for guidance will find its evidences therein, whoever is looking for salvation may find that I have explained the way to it in this book, whoever desires to follow the track of the Prophets, Messengers and righteous people will find their path herein while those who turn away from their way only befool themselves and take to the straying path.

It is a matter of fact that adherents of each religion call others to it and believe that truth only abide in their

---

[1] Al-Ahqâf 46:35
[2] Aal 'Imrân 3:200

religion. It is also a fact that adherents of each belief
call others to follow their leader and extol him. As for
Muslim, he does not call people to follow his ideology.
His religion is the religion of Allâh with which He is
pleased. Allâh says:

﴿إِنَّ ٱلدِّينَ عِندَ ٱللَّهِ ٱلْإِسْلَٰمُ﴾

"Truly, the religion with Allâh is Islâm" [1]

He also does not call people to glorify a human being,
for all human beings are equal in the Religion of Allâh;
nothing distinguishes one from another except piety.
A Muslim rather calls people to follow the path of
their Lord, to believe in His Messengers and follow
His Law which He revealed to the last of His
Messengers Muhammad ﷺ and which He
commanded him to convey to all mankind.

It's on this account that I wrote this book in order to
call people to the Religion of Allâh which He is
pleased with and with which He sent His Last
Messenger ﷺ in order to guide those who are
looking for guidance and happiness. By Allâh! No
human being can have real happiness except through
this religion and none can have rest of mind except by
believing that Allâh is the only Lord (worthy of
worship), that Muhammad is His Messenger and that
Islâm is the only acceptable religion of Allâh.

Thousands of those who embraced Islâm have testified
that they did not know real life until after they
embraced Islâm and that they did never tasted

---

[1] Aal 'Imrân 3:19

happiness except under the shade of Islâm. Since it is a fact that every human being looks for happiness, peace of mind and truth, I prepare this work to help them achieve that. I pray that Allâh makes this work purely for His sake and let it be well-accepted and make it one of those righteous deeds that will benefit its doer in this world and the next.

I equally request from whoever has any observation or correction either on the Arabic text of this Book or any of its translated versions to kindly send it to me through the below-mentioned address.

All praise is due to Allâh firstly and lastly, outwardly and inwardly. All praise is due to Him publicly and secretly. All praise is due to Him in the beginning and the end. All praise is due to him as much as can fill the heavens and the earth and whatever else that Our Lord may wish. May Allâh bestow peace and much blessing on our Prophet Muhammad ﷺ, his Companions and all those who follow his path till the day of reckoning.

The author,

**Dr. Muhammad bin Abdullah
bin Saalih As-Suhaym**
Riyadh 13-10-1420
P. O. Box 261032
Riyadh 1342 and
P. O. Box 6249
Riyadh 11442

Where is the Way?

When man grows and starts understanding things, many questions come to his mind like: Where am I from? What will be my end? Who created me and the universe around me? Who owns and controls this universe? And other questions like these.

However, he is unable to provide himself with answers to these questions. Even modern science is not capable of providing answers to them because these issues fall within religious domains. That is why there are numerous narrations and different superstitions and tales about them that only add to man's confusion and distress. It is impossible for man to get a satisfying answer to these questions unless he is guided by Allâh to the true religion that is capable of providing final decision on these and similar issues; for, these issues are among the divine secrets that only the true religion can give correct and accurate answers to and that is the only religion that Allâh revealed to His Prophets and Messengers. It is then incumbent upon man to learn the true religion and have belief in it in order to have his confusion and doubts removed and in order to be guided to the Straight Path.

In the following pages, I invite you to follow the Straight Path of Allâh and I present to you some evidences and proofs that you may carefully and patiently reflect on.

Existence of Allâh, His Lordship (Over All Creation)

Many people do worship man-made deities like trees, stones and even human beings; that is why the Jews and idolaters asked the Messenger of Allâh ﷺ about the characteristics of his Lord. In reply to this question Allâh revealed:

﴿قُلْ هُوَ ٱللَّهُ أَحَدٌ ٠ ٱللَّهُ ٱلصَّمَدُ ٠ لَمْ يَلِدْ وَلَمْ يُولَدْ ٠ وَلَمْ يَكُن لَّهُۥ كُفُوًا أَحَدٌۢ﴾

"Say (O Muhammad): He is Allâh, (the) One, Allâh, the Self-Sufficient Master (Whom all creatures need, He neither eats nor drinks). He begets not nor is He begotten. And there is none co-equal or comparable unto Him."[1]

He also says:

﴿إِنَّ رَبَّكُمُ ٱللَّهُ ٱلَّذِى خَلَقَ ٱلسَّمَـٰوَٰتِ وَٱلْأَرْضَ فِى سِتَّةِ أَيَّامٍ ثُمَّ ٱسْتَوَىٰ عَلَى ٱلْعَرْشِ يُغْشِى ٱلَّيْلَ ٱلنَّهَارَ يَطْلُبُهُۥ حَثِيثًا وَٱلشَّمْسَ وَٱلْقَمَرَ وَٱلنُّجُومَ مُسَخَّرَٰتٍ بِأَمْرِهِۦٓ أَلَا لَهُ ٱلْخَلْقُ وَٱلْأَمْرُ تَبَارَكَ ٱللَّهُ رَبُّ ٱلْعَـٰلَمِينَ﴾

"Indeed your Lord is Allâh Who created the heavens and the earth in Six Days and then He Istawa (rose over) the Throne (really in a manner that suits His Majesty). He brings night as a cover over the day, seeking it rapidly, and (He created) the sun, the moon, the stars subjected to His Command. Blessed be Allâh, the Lord of all the worlds!"[2]

---

[1] Al-Ikhlâs 112: 1-4.
[2] Al-A'raaf 7:54.

He also says:

$$﴿ٱللَّهُ ٱلَّذِى رَفَعَ ٱلسَّمَٰوَٰتِ بِغَيْرِ عَمَدٍ تَرَوْنَهَا ۖ ثُمَّ ٱسْتَوَىٰ عَلَى ٱلْعَرْشِ ۖ وَسَخَّرَ ٱلشَّمْسَ وَٱلْقَمَرَ ۖ كُلٌّ يَجْرِى لِأَجَلٍ مُّسَمًّى ۚ يُدَبِّرُ ٱلْأَمْرَ يُفَصِّلُ ٱلْآيَٰتِ لَعَلَّكُم بِلِقَآءِ رَبِّكُمْ تُوقِنُونَ ۝ وَهُوَ ٱلَّذِى مَدَّ ٱلْأَرْضَ وَجَعَلَ فِيهَا رَوَٰسِىَ وَأَنْهَٰرًا ۖ وَمِن كُلِّ ٱلثَّمَرَٰتِ جَعَلَ فِيهَا زَوْجَيْنِ ٱثْنَيْنِ ۖ يُغْشِى ٱلَّيْلَ ٱلنَّهَارَ ۚ إِنَّ فِى ذَٰلِكَ لَآيَٰتٍ لِّقَوْمٍ يَتَفَكَّرُونَ ۝ ٱللَّهُ يَعْلَمُ مَا تَحْمِلُ كُلُّ أُنثَىٰ وَمَا تَغِيضُ ٱلْأَرْحَامُ وَمَا تَزْدَادُ ۖ وَكُلُّ شَىْءٍ عِندَهُ بِمِقْدَارٍ ۝ عَٰلِمُ ٱلْغَيْبِ وَٱلشَّهَٰدَةِ ٱلْكَبِيرُ ٱلْمُتَعَالِ ۝ ﴾$$

"Allâh is He, Who raised the heaven without pillars that you can see. Then He Istawa (rose above) the Throne (really in a manner that suits His Majesty). He has subjected the sun and the moon (to continue going round)! Each running (its course) for a term appointed. He regulates all affairs, explaining the Aayaat (proofs, evidences, verses, lessons, signs, revelations, etc.) in detail, that you may believe with certainty in the meeting with your Lord. And it is He who spread out the earth, and placed therein firm mountains and rivers and of every kind of fruits He made in pairs. He brings the night as a cover over the day..." until He says: "Allâh knows what every female bears and how much the womb falls short (of their time or number) or exceed. Everything with Him is in due proportion. All-Knower of the unseen and the seen, the Most Great, the Most-High."[1]

Allâh also says:

$$﴿قُلْ مَن رَّبُّ ٱلسَّمَٰوَٰتِ وَٱلْأَرْضِ قُلِ ٱللَّهُ ۚ قُلْ أَفَٱتَّخَذْتُم مِّن دُونِهِۦ أَوْلِيَآءَ لَا$$

---

[1] Ar-Râ'd 13:2, 3, 8, 9.

$$يَمۡلِكُونَ لِأَنفُسِهِمۡ نَفۡعًا وَلَا ضَرًّا قُلۡ هَلۡ يَسۡتَوِى ٱلۡأَعۡمَىٰ وَٱلۡبَصِيرُ أَمۡ هَلۡ تَسۡتَوِى ٱلظُّلُمَـٰتُ وَٱلنُّورُ أَمۡ جَعَلُوا۟ لِلَّهِ شُرَكَآءَ خَلَقُوا۟ كَخَلۡقِهِۦ فَتَشَـٰبَهَ ٱلۡخَلۡقُ عَلَيۡهِمۡ قُلِ ٱللَّهُ خَـٰلِقُ كُلِّ شَىۡءٍ وَهُوَ ٱلۡوَٰحِدُ ٱلۡقَهَّـٰرُ$$

"Say (O Muhammad ﷺ): Who is the Lord of the heavens and the earth? Say: (It is) Allâh. Say: Have you then taken (for worship) protectors other than Him, such as have no power either for benefit or for harm to themselves? Say: Is the blind equal to the one who sees? Or darkness equal to light? Or do they assign Allâh partners who created the like of His creation, so that the creation (which they made and His creation) seemed alike to them? Say: Allâh is the Creator of all things. He is the One, the Irresistible."[1]

While establishing for mankind His signs as evidences and proofs, He says:

$$وَمِنۡ ءَايَـٰتِهِ ٱلَّيۡلُ وَٱلنَّهَارُ وَٱلشَّمۡسُ وَٱلۡقَمَرُ لَا تَسۡجُدُوا۟ لِلشَّمۡسِ وَلَا لِلۡقَمَرِ وَٱسۡجُدُوا۟ لِلَّهِ ٱلَّذِى خَلَقَهُنَّ إِن كُنتُمۡ إِيَّاهُ تَعۡبُدُونَ ○ فَإِنِ ٱسۡتَكۡبَرُوا۟ فَٱلَّذِينَ عِندَ رَبِّكَ يُسَبِّحُونَ لَهُۥ بِٱلَّيۡلِ وَٱلنَّهَارِ وَهُمۡ لَا يَسۡـَٔمُونَ ○ وَمِنۡ ءَايَـٰتِهِۦٓ أَنَّكَ تَرَى ٱلۡأَرۡضَ خَـٰشِعَةً فَإِذَآ أَنزَلۡنَا عَلَيۡهَا ٱلۡمَآءَ ٱهۡتَزَّتۡ وَرَبَتۡ إِنَّ ٱلَّذِىٓ أَحۡيَاهَا لَمُحۡىِ ٱلۡمَوۡتَىٰٓ إِنَّهُۥ عَلَىٰ كُلِّ شَىۡءٍ قَدِيرٌ$$

"And from among His signs are the night and the day, and the sun and the moon. Prostrate not to the sun nor the moon, but prostrate to Allâh who created them, if you really worship Him. But if they are too

---
[1] Ar-Ra'd 13:16

proud (to do so), then those who are with your Lord (angels) glorify Him night and day, and never are they tired. And among His signs (in this), that you see the earth barren, but when We send down water (rain) to it, it is stirred to life and growth (of vegetations). Verily, He Who gives it life, sure is Able to give life to the dead (on the Day of Resurrection). Indeed He is Able to do all things.''[1]

He also says:

وَمِنْ ءَايَـٰتِهِۦ خَلْقُ ٱلسَّمَـٰوَٰتِ وَٱلْأَرْضِ وَٱخْتِلَـٰفُ أَلْسِنَتِكُمْ وَأَلْوَٰنِكُمْ إِنَّ فِى ذَٰلِكَ لَآيَـٰتٍ لِّلْعَـٰلِمِينَ ○ وَمِنْ ءَايَـٰتِهِۦ مَنَامُكُم بِٱلَّيْلِ وَٱلنَّهَارِ وَٱبْتِغَآؤُكُم مِّن فَضْلِهِۦٓ إِنَّ فِى ذَٰلِكَ لَآيَـٰتٍ لِّقَوْمٍ يَسْمَعُونَ ﴾

"And among His signs is the creation of the heavens and the earth, and the differences of your languages and colours. Verily, in that are indeed signs for men of sound knowledge. And among His signs are the sleep that you take by night and by day...''[2]

While describing Himself with attributes of beauty and perfection He says:

﴿ٱللَّهُ لَآ إِلَـٰهَ إِلَّا هُوَ ٱلْحَىُّ ٱلْقَيُّومُ لَا تَأْخُذُهُۥ سِنَةٌ وَلَا نَوْمٌ لَّهُۥ مَا فِى ٱلسَّمَـٰوَٰتِ وَمَا فِى ٱلْأَرْضِ مَن ذَا ٱلَّذِى يَشْفَعُ عِندَهُۥٓ إِلَّا بِإِذْنِهِۦ يَعْلَمُ مَا بَيْنَ أَيْدِيهِمْ وَمَا خَلْفَهُمْ وَلَا يُحِيطُونَ بِشَىْءٍ مِّنْ عِلْمِهِۦٓ إِلَّا بِمَا شَآءَ﴾

"Allâh! None has the right to be worshipped but He. The Ever-Living, the One Who sustains and protects all that exists. Neither slumber nor sleep overtakes Him. To Him belongs whatsoever is in the heavens

---

[1] Fussilat 41:37-39

[2] Ar-Rûm 30:22-23

*and whatsoever is in the earth. Who is he that can
intercede with Him except with His permission? He
knows what happens to them (His creatures) in this
world and what will happen to them in the Hereafter.
And they will never compass anything of His
knowledge except that which He wills."*[1]

He also says:

﴿غَافِرِ ٱلذَّنۢبِ وَقَابِلِ ٱلتَّوْبِ شَدِيدِ ٱلْعِقَابِ ذِى ٱلطَّوْلِ لَآ إِلَٰهَ إِلَّا هُوَ
إِلَيْهِ ٱلْمَصِيرُ﴾

*"The Forgiver of sins, the Acceptor of repentance, the
Stern in punishment, the Bestower (of favours). None
has the right to be worshipped but He. To Him is the
final return."*[2]

He - may His praise be exalted - also says:

﴿هُوَ ٱللَّهُ ٱلَّذِى لَآ إِلَٰهَ إِلَّا هُوَ ٱلْمَلِكُ ٱلْقُدُّوسُ ٱلسَّلَٰمُ ٱلْمُؤْمِنُ
ٱلْمُهَيْمِنُ ٱلْعَزِيزُ ٱلْجَبَّارُ ٱلْمُتَكَبِّرُ سُبْحَٰنَ ٱللَّهِ عَمَّا يُشْرِكُونَ﴾

*"He is Allâh, besides Whom none has the right to be
worshipped, the King, the Holy, the One free from all
defects, the Giver of security, the Watcher over His
creatures, the All-Mighty, the Compeller, the
Supreme. Glory be to Allâh! (High is He) above all
that they associate as partners with Him."*[3]

This wise and Omnipotent Lord who made Himself
known to His slaves and established for them His
signs and proofs and described Himself with attributes

---

[1] Al-Baqarah 2:255
[2] Ghâfir 40:3
[3] Al-Hashr 59:23

of perfection had prophetic ordainments, human wisdom and nature testify to His existence, to His Lordship and being the only one having the right to be worshipped. I will - God willing - show that to you in the following pages.

As for proofs of His existence and Lordship, they are:

One: Creation of This Universe and Its Wonderful Design

O man! All this universe that surrounds you; the heavens, the stars, the galaxies and the earth that is spread in which there are neighbouring tracts out of which different plants grow bearing all fruits, and on which you find all creatures in pairs... this universe did not create itself and could never create itself. It must then have a creator. Who then is that creator who created it in this wonderful design and perfection and made it a sign for those who can see save Allâh the One, the Subduer Whom there is no Lord or deity worthy of worship beside Him. He says:

$$﴿أَمْ خُلِقُوا مِنْ غَيْرِ شَيْءٍ أَمْ هُمُ ٱلْخَٰلِقُونَ ٥ أَمْ خَلَقُوا ٱلسَّمَٰوَٰتِ وَٱلْأَرْضَ بَل لَّا يُوقِنُونَ ﴾$$

"Were they created by nothing or were they themselves the creators? Or did they create the heavens and the earth? Nay, but they have no firm belief."[1]

These two Verses imply three questions:

1- Were they created from nothing?

---

[1] At-Tûr 52:35-36

2- Did they create themselves?

3- Did they create the heavens and the earth?

If their creation was not accidental and they had not created themselves or created the heavens and the earth; it should then be affirmed that there exists a creator who created them as well as the heavens and the earth. That Creator is Allâh, the One, the Subduer.

Two: The Nature

All creatures are naturally inclined to believe in the existence of the Creator; to affirm that He is greater and mightier than all things. This inclination is more well-rooted in the nature than elementary mathematics and does not need to be proved by any evidence except for him who has an abnormal nature; a nature that has been exposed to circumstances that turn it away from what it should admit.[1] Allâh says:

﴿فَأَقِمْ وَجْهَكَ لِلدِّينِ حَنِيفًا فِطْرَتَ اللَّهِ الَّتِي فَطَرَ النَّاسَ عَلَيْهَا لَا تَبْدِيلَ لِخَلْقِ اللَّهِ ذَلِكَ الدِّينُ الْقَيِّمُ وَلَكِنَّ أَكْثَرَ النَّاسِ لَا يَعْلَمُونَ﴾

"That (Islâmic Monotheism) is the nature upon which Allâh has created mankind. Let there be no change in Allâh's (law of) creation. That is the straight religion."[2]

The Messenger of Allâh said:

«كُلُّ مَوْلُودٍ يُولَدُ عَلَى الفِطْرَةِ فَأبواهُ يُهَوِّدَانِهِ أَوْ يُنَصِّرَانِهِ أَوْ

---
[1] *Majmoo' Fatawa Ibn Taymiyah* 1:47-49
[2] Ar-Rûm 30:30

يُمَجِّسانِهِ، كَمَثَلِ البَهِيمَةِ تُنْتَجُ البَهِيمَةَ، هَلْ تَرَى فِيها جَدْعاءَ؟ثُمَّ يَقُولُ أَبوهُرَيرَةَ اقْرَءُوا إن شِئْتُمْ:

﴿فِطْرَتَ ٱللَّهِ ٱلَّتِى فَطَرَ ٱلنَّاسَ عَلَيْهَا لَا تَبْدِيلَ لِخَلْقِ ٱللَّهِ ذَٰلِكَ ٱلدِّينُ ٱلْقَيِّمُ﴾

"Every child is born with natural inclination to Islâmic Monotheism and it is his parents who make him a Jew, a Christian or a Magian[1] just as the animal gives birth to its young whole, wherein you find no mutilation." Then Aboo Hurayrah (who is the narrator of this hadeeth) said: "Recite if you like (Allâh's words): "That (Islâmic Monotheism) is the nature upon which Allâh has created mankind. Let there be no change in Allâh's (law of) creation. That is the straight religion."'[2]

He also said:

«أَلَا! إِنَّ رَبِّي أَمَرَنِي أَنْ أُعَلِّمَكُمْ مَا جَهِلْتُمْ مِمَّا عَلَّمَنِي، يَوْمِي هَذَا، كُلُّ مَالٍ نَحَلْتُهُ عَبْدًا، حَلَالٌ، وَإِنِّي خَلَقْتُ عِبَادِي حُنَفَاءَ كُلَّهُمْ، وَإِنَّهُمْ أَتَتْهُمُ الشَّيَاطِينُ فَاجْتَالَتْهُمْ عَنْ دِينِهِمْ، وَحَرَّمَتْ عَلَيْهِمْ مَا أَحْلَلْتُ لَهُمْ، وَأَمَرَتْهُمْ أَنْ يُشْرِكُوا بِي مَا لَمْ أُنْزِلْ بِهِ سُلْطَانًا»

"Verily, my Lord commanded me to teach you what you do not know of what He has taught me today: 'All money that I endow a slave with is lawful (for him). I created my slaves naturally inclined to Islâmic

---

[1] Magians are those who worship fire and other natural phenomena. (AA)

[2] Al-Bukhari (1385) and Muslim (2658)

*Monotheism and it were the devils who came to them,
led them away from their religion, made forbidden for
them what I made lawful and enjoined on them to
associate partners with Me in worship of which I did
not send any proof.'* ''[1]

Three: Consensus of All People

All past and modern nations are in consensus that this
universe has a creator who is Allâh the Lord of all the
worlds, that He is the Creator of the heavens and the
earth and that He has no partner among His creatures
as He does not have a partner in His Sovereignty.

No belief has ever been reported from any of the past
nations that their false deities took part with Allâh in
the creation of the heavens and the earth. Rather, they
all believed that it was Allâh Who created them and
their gods, that there was no creator or sustainer
besides Him and that He alone owns the power to
benefit or harm.[2] Allâh informs us in the following
Verses of the idolaters' affirmation of His Lordship
and guardianship:

﴿وَلَئِن سَأَلْتَهُم مَّنْ خَلَقَ ٱلسَّمَٰوَٰتِ وَٱلْأَرْضَ وَسَخَّرَ ٱلشَّمْسَ وَٱلْقَمَرَ
لَيَقُولُنَّ ٱللَّهُ فَأَنَّىٰ يُؤْفَكُونَ ٠ ٱللَّهُ يَبْسُطُ ٱلرِّزْقَ لِمَن يَشَآءُ مِنْ عِبَادِهِ وَيَقْدِرُ
لَهُۥٓ إِنَّ ٱللَّهَ بِكُلِّ شَىْءٍ عَلِيمٌ ٠ وَلَئِن سَأَلْتَهُم مَّن نَّزَّلَ مِنَ ٱلسَّمَآءِ مَآءً
فَأَحْيَا بِهِ ٱلْأَرْضَ مِنۢ بَعْدِ مَوْتِهَا لَيَقُولُنَّ ٱللَّهُ قُلِ ٱلْحَمْدُ لِلَّهِ بَلْ
أَكْثَرُهُمْ لَا يَعْقِلُونَ﴾

*"If you were to ask them: 'Who has created the
heavens and the earth and subjected the sun and the*

---

[1] Ahmad (4/162) and Muslim (2865)
[2] *Majmoo' Fatawa* 14:380-383

*moon?' They will surely reply: 'Allâh'. How then are
they deviating (as polytheists and disbelievers)? Allâh
enlarges the provision for whom He wills of His slaves
and straitens it for whom (He wills). Verily, Allâh is
the All-Knower of everything. If you were to ask them:
'Who sends down water (rain) from the sky and gives
life therewith to earth after its death?' They will surely
reply: 'Allâh'. Say: 'All the praises and thanks be to
Allâh!' Nay! Most of them have no sense.''*[1]

وَلَئِن سَأَلْتَهُم مَّنْ خَلَقَ ٱلسَّمَٰوَٰتِ وَٱلْأَرْضَ لَيَقُولُنَّ خَلَقَهُنَّ ٱلْعَزِيزُ ٱلْعَلِيمُ ﴾

*"And indeed if you ask them, 'Who has created the
heavens and the earth?' They will surely say: 'The
All-Mighty, the All-Knower created them.' ''*[2]

Four: The Reason

Human reason inevitably confirms that this universe
has a great Creator; for the sound reason agrees that
this universe is a created thing that did not bring itself
to being, hence, it must have an originator.

Also, man knows that he falls into crises and afflictions
and when he is unable to prevent them or remove
them, he faces the heavens with his heart and seeks for
His Lord's aid to remove his distress even though he
may denounce his Lord and worship his idols in his
normal days. This is an undisputable fact. Even the
animal raises his head up and looks at the sky
whenever it is visited by an affliction. The Almighty

[1] Al-'Ankabût 29:61-63
[2] Az-Zukhruf 43:9

Allâh informs us that man, whenever he is afflicted with harm, hastens to his Lord and asks Him to remove the harm. Allâh says,

﴿وَإِذَا مَسَّ ٱلْإِنسَٰنَ ضُرٌّ دَعَا رَبَّهُ مُنِيبًا إِلَيْهِ ثُمَّ إِذَا خَوَّلَهُ نِعْمَةً مِّنْهُ نَسِيَ مَا كَانَ يَدْعُوٓاْ إِلَيْهِ مِن قَبْلُ وَجَعَلَ لِلَّهِ أَندَادًا﴾

"And when some hurt touches man, he cries to his Lord (Allâh Alone) turning to Him in repentance, but when He bestows a favour upon him from Himself, he forgets that for which he cried for before and he sets up rivals to Allâh."[1]

He also says about the idolaters:

﴿هُوَ ٱلَّذِى يُسَيِّرُكُمْ فِى ٱلْبَرِّ وَٱلْبَحْرِ حَتَّىٰٓ إِذَا كُنتُمْ فِى ٱلْفُلْكِ وَجَرَيْنَ بِهِم بِرِيحٍ طَيِّبَةٍ وَفَرِحُواْ بِهَا جَآءَتْهَا رِيحٌ عَاصِفٌ وَجَآءَهُمُ ٱلْمَوْجُ مِن كُلِّ مَكَانٍ وَظَنُّوٓاْ أَنَّهُمْ أُحِيطَ بِهِمْ دَعَوُاْ ٱللَّهَ مُخْلِصِينَ لَهُ ٱلدِّينَ لَئِنْ أَنجَيْتَنَا مِنْ هَٰذِهِ لَنَكُونَنَّ مِنَ ٱلشَّٰكِرِينَ ۞ فَلَمَّآ أَنجَىٰهُمْ إِذَا هُمْ يَبْغُونَ فِى ٱلْأَرْضِ بِغَيْرِ ٱلْحَقِّ يَٰٓأَيُّهَا ٱلنَّاسُ إِنَّمَا بَغْيُكُمْ عَلَىٰٓ أَنفُسِكُم مَّتَٰعَ ٱلْحَيَوٰةِ ٱلدُّنْيَا ثُمَّ إِلَيْنَا مَرْجِعُكُمْ فَنُنَبِّئُكُم بِمَا كُنتُمْ تَعْمَلُونَ ۞﴾

"He it is Who enables you to travel through land and sea, till when you are in the ships and they sail with them with a favourable wind, and they are glad therein, then comes a stormy wind and the waves come to them from all sides and they think that they are circled therein, they invoke Allâh, making their faith pure for Him Alone, saying: 'If You (Allâh) deliver us from this, we shall truly be of the grateful. But when He delivered them, behold! They rebel

---

[1] Az-Zumar 39:8

(disobey Allâh) in the earth wrongfully. O mankind! Your rebellion (disobedience to Allâh) is only against your own selves, - a brief enjoyment of this worldly life, then (in the end) unto Us is your return and We shall inform you that which you used to do.' ''[1]

He also says:

وَإِذَا غَشِيَهُم مَّوْجٌ كَالظُّلَلِ دَعَوُا اللَّهَ مُخْلِصِينَ لَهُ الدِّينَ فَلَمَّا نَجَّنَهُمْ إِلَى الْبَرِّ فَمِنْهُم مُّقْتَصِدٌ وَمَا يَجْحَدُ بِآيَنِنَآ إِلَّا كُلُّ خَتَّارٍ كَفُورٍ

"And when a wave covers them like shades (i.e., like clouds or the mountains of seawater) they invoke Allâh, making their invocations for Him only. But when he brings them safe to land, there are among them those that stop in the middle (between belief and disbelief). But none denies Our Signs but every perfidious ungrateful."[2]

This Lord who brought this universe to existence, created man in the best form, embedded in his nature servitude and submission to Him, subjected human reason to His Lordship and His exclusive worthiness to be worshipped. It is Allâh Whom all nations unanimously testify to His guardianship... as He should inevitably be One in His Lordship and worthiness to be worshipped. As He has no partner in creating His creatures, He should also have no partner in His worthiness to be worshipped. There are numerous evidences for this,[3] some of which are:

---

[1] Yûnus 10:22-23
[2] Luqmân 31:32
[3] For more of these evidences, see *Kitaabut-Tawheed* by Muhammad Ibn Abdul Wahhaab.

1- There is only in this universe one God Who is the
creator and the sustainer of all. None brings harm
or benefit except Him. Had there been any other
god besides Him, that god would have had his own
work, creation and command and none of both
would have allowed another to share the creation
with him. Hence, one of them must have overpowered and subdued the other. In that case, the
subdued could not have been a god and the
Subduer should be the real God with whom none
can share the right to be worshipped just as none
shares with Him His guardianship and lordship.
Allâh says:

﴿مَا ٱتَّخَذَ ٱللَّهُ مِن وَلَدٍ وَمَا كَانَ مَعَهُ مِنْ إِلَٰهٍ إِذًا لَّذَهَبَ كُلُّ إِلَٰهٍ
بِمَا خَلَقَ وَلَعَلَا بَعْضُهُمْ عَلَىٰ بَعْضٍ سُبْحَٰنَ ٱللَّهِ عَمَّا يَصِفُونَ﴾

*"No son (or offspring or children) did Allâh beget, nor
is there any god along with Him; (if there had been
many gods), behold, each god would have taken away
what he had created, and some would have tried to
overcome others! Glorified be Allâh above all that they
attribute to Him."*[1]

2- None deserves to be worshipped but Allâh Who
created the heavens and the earth; for, man seeks to
gain the favour of the Lord Who brings him benefit
and prevents harm, evils and calamities from him
and none but the one who owns the heavens and
the earth is capable of doing all these. Let those
who are searching for the truth read:

﴿قُلِ ٱدْعُوا۟ ٱلَّذِينَ زَعَمْتُم مِّن دُونِ ٱللَّهِ لَا يَمْلِكُونَ مِثْقَالَ ذَرَّةٍ فِى

---

[1] Al-Mu'minûn 23:91

ٱلسَّمَوَتِ وَلَا فِى ٱلْأَرْضِ وَمَا لَهُمْ فِيهِمَا مِن شِرْكٍ وَمَا لَهُ مِنْهُم مِّن ظَهِيرٍ ۞ وَلَا تَنفَعُ ٱلشَّفَعَةُ عِندَهُ إِلَّا لِمَنْ أَذِنَ لَهُ ۞

"Say (O Muhammad ﷺ) (to those polytheists, pagans, etc.) 'Call upon those whom you assert (to be associate gods) besides Allâh, they possess not even the weight of an atom (or small ant), - either in the heavens or on the earth nor have they any share in either, nor there is for Him any supporter from among them. Intercession with Him profits not, except for him whom He permits.' "[1]

These Verses and others sever heart's affinity to other things besides Allâh through four factors:

One: That those whom the polytheists worship possess not even the weight of an atom with Allâh, and he who possesses not a weight of an atom cannot benefit nor harm and therefore, is not worthy of being worshipped or being taken as Allâh's associate in worship. It is Allâh alone Who owns them and controls them.

Two: That they possess nothing in the heavens and the earth and they do not even have an atom weight of share in them.

Three: Allâh has no helper among His creatures. Rather, He is the One who helps them in what is of benefit for them and drives away from them what harms them. For, He completely has no need of them; it is they who are rather in absolute need of Him.

Four: That these so-called associates are not capable of

---

[1] Saba' 34:22-23

interceding with Allâh on behalf of their followers and
they will not even be given permission to do so. Allâh
does not give permission to intercede except to His
friends, and His friends also can not intercede except
on behalf of the one whom Allâh is pleased with his
sayings, deeds and belief.[1]

3- Systematic arrangement and precise execution of
   the affairs of this universe is the strongest indication that its controller is one Lord, one (King),
   beside Whom there is no other creator. As it is
   impossible for this universe to have two creators, so
   it is impossible for it to have two Lords. Allâh says:

$$﴿لَوْ كَانَ فِيهِمَآ ءَالِهَةٌ إِلَّا ٱللَّهُ لَفَسَدَتَا فَسُبْحَٰنَ ٱللَّهِ رَبِّ ٱلْعَرْشِ عَمَّا يَصِفُونَ﴾$$

*"Had there been therein (in the heavens and the earth)
gods besides Allâh, then verily both would have been
ruined."*[2]

Had it been assumed that there was in the heaven and
the earth another god besides Allâh, they would have
been ruined. Because, had there been another god
besides Allâh, both would need to be autocratic and
have right of free disposal. That would have then lead
to contention and fighting and the ruin of the heaven
and the earth would have occurred as a result. It is
impossible for the body to have two controlling souls;
if that happens the body will be destroyed - how then
can it be imagined that this universe which is greater,
should have two lords?

---

[1] See *Qurratu 'uyoonil-muwahhideen* p.100
[2] Al-Anbiyâ' 21:22

4- Consensus of the Prophets and Messengers: All
nations agree that the Prophets and Messengers are
the wisest, most intelligent, best in morality, most
sincere, most knowledgeable of what Allâh wants
and the most rightly guided of all people, because,
they received revelation from Allâh and conveyed
it to people. And all Prophets and Messengers -
right from Adam to the last Prophet who is
Muhammad, peace be upon them all - have all
called their peoples to the belief in Allâh and
abstention from worshipping anything besides
Him and that He is the only True Lord. Allâh says:

﴿وَمَآ أَرْسَلْنَا مِن قَبْلِكَ مِن رَّسُولٍ إِلَّا نُوحِىٓ إِلَيْهِ أَنَّهُ لَآ إِلَٰهَ إِلَّآ أَنَا۠ فَٱعْبُدُونِ﴾

*"And We did not send any Messenger before you (O
Muhammad ﷺ) but We revealed to him saying: None
has the right to be worshipped but I (Allâh), so
worship Me (Alone)."*[1]

He also says about Nooh - Peace be upon him - that he
told his people,

﴿أَن لَّا تَعْبُدُوٓا۟ إِلَّا ٱللَّهَ إِنِّىٓ أَخَافُ عَلَيْكُمْ عَذَابَ يَوْمٍ أَلِيمٍ﴾

*"That you worship none but Allâh, surely, I fear for
you the torment of a painful Day."*[2]

He - may He be glorified- also says about the last of all
Messengers, Muhammad ﷺ,

﴿قُلْ إِنَّمَا يُوحَىٰٓ إِلَىَّ أَنَّمَآ إِلَٰهُكُمْ إِلَٰهٌ وَٰحِدٌ فَهَلْ أَنتُم

---
[1] Al-Anbiyâ' 21:25
[2] Hûd 11:26

مُّسْلِمُونَ ﴾

*"Say (O Muhammad ﷺ): It is revealed to me that
your Ilah (God) is only one Ilah (God - Allâh). Will
you then submit to His Will (become Muslims and
stop worshipping others besides Allâh)?"*[1]

This God is the One who wonderfully created the
universe from naught; He created man in the best form
and perfected his creation and impressed in his nature
the affirmation of His Lordship and His exclusive right
to be worshipped. He lets him have peace of mind
through his submission to Him and following His Path
and He ordained it on his soul not to be at rest until it
surrenders to its Creator and be in continuous contact
with Him. He also makes it impossible to contact with
Him except through His Straight Path which the
honourable Prophets conveyed. He gave man
intelligence which only becomes upright and
functions properly when he believes in Allâh, Glory
be to Him.

When one has an upright nature, a peaceful soul and a
believing heart, one achieves happiness, security and
peace in this world and the Hereafter. But when man
refuses all that, he will live in the alleys of this world
disorganised and divided among its gods, ignorant as
to who can benefit him or prevent harm from him. It is
in order that true faith may be established in the heart
and the ugliness of disbelief may be exposed that
Allâh makes a parable - for parables bring meanings
closer to understanding. He makes a parable of a man

---
[1] Al-Anbiyâ' 21:108

whose affair is divided between numerous gods and a man who worships his Lord alone. He, may He be glorified, says,

﴿ضَرَبَ ٱللَّهُ مَثَلًا رَّجُلًا فِيهِ شُرَكَآءُ مُتَشَٰكِسُونَ وَرَجُلًا سَلَمًا لِّرَجُلٍ هَلْ يَسْتَوِيَانِ مَثَلًا ٱلْحَمْدُ لِلَّهِ بَلْ أَكْثَرُهُمْ لَا يَعْلَمُونَ﴾

"Allâh puts forth a similitude: a (slave) man belonging to many partners (like those who worship others along with Allâh) disputing with one another, and a (slave) man belonging entirely to one master (like those who worship Allâh Alone). Are those two equal in comparison? All the praises and thanks are to Allâh! But most of them know not."[1]

Allâh likens the slave who is a polytheist to a slave who is owned by different associates and over whom they all contend with each other. He is divided among them and everyone of them directs him and assigns responsibilities to him. He is confused among them and is always unstable. He is unable to satisfy their different and contradicting desires that tear his energy and directions apart.

He also likens the slave who is a monotheist to a slave who is owned by a single master. He knows what his master wants and the assignments he gives him. He is thereby comfortable and settled on a clear path. Both of these two slaves cannot be equal. For, one submits to a single master and enjoys the pleasure of uprightness, knowledge and certainty and the other one submits to different and disputing masters and is thereby punished and distressed. He is not stable on a

---
[1] Az-Zumar 39:29

condition and cannot please even one of them let alone all of them.

After proofs on the existence of Allâh, His Lordship and His exclusive right to be worshipped have become clear, we should then acquaint ourselves with His creation of the universe and man, and know His wisdom behind that.

Creation of the Universe

This universe with its heavens, earth, stars, galaxies, seas, trees and all living things are created from non-existence by Allâh - the Glorified and Exalted. He says,

﴿قُلْ أَئِنَّكُمْ لَتَكْفُرُونَ بِالَّذِى خَلَقَ ٱلْأَرْضَ فِى يَوْمَيْنِ وَتَجْعَلُونَ لَهُۥٓ أَندَادًا ذَٰلِكَ رَبُّ ٱلْعَٰلَمِينَ ۝ وَجَعَلَ فِيهَا رَوَٰسِيَ مِن فَوْقِهَا وَبَٰرَكَ فِيهَا وَقَدَّرَ فِيهَآ أَقْوَٰتَهَا فِىٓ أَرْبَعَةِ أَيَّامٍ سَوَآءً لِّلسَّآئِلِينَ ۝ ثُمَّ ٱسْتَوَىٰٓ إِلَى ٱلسَّمَآءِ وَهِىَ دُخَانٌ فَقَالَ لَهَا وَلِلْأَرْضِ ٱئْتِيَا طَوْعًا أَوْ كَرْهًا قَالَتَآ أَتَيْنَا طَآئِعِينَ ۝ فَقَضَىٰهُنَّ سَبْعَ سَمَٰوَاتٍ فِى يَوْمَيْنِ وَأَوْحَىٰ فِى كُلِّ سَمَآءٍ أَمْرَهَا وَزَيَّنَّا ٱلسَّمَآءَ ٱلدُّنْيَا بِمَصَٰبِيحَ وَحِفْظًا ذَٰلِكَ تَقْدِيرُ ٱلْعَزِيزِ ٱلْعَلِيمِ﴾

"Say (O Muhammad): Do you verily disbelieve in Him Who created the earth in two days and you set up rivals (in worship) with Him? That is Lord of the worlds. He placed therein (i.e., the earth) firm mountains from above it, and He blessed it, and measured therein its sustenance (for its dwellers) in four days equal (i.e., all these four 'days' are equal in the length of time) for all those who ask about (its creation). Then He rose over towards the heaven when it was smoke, and said to it and to the earth, 'Come both of you willingly or unwillingly!' They both said, 'We come, willingly.' Then He completed and finished from the creation (as) seven heavens in two days and He made in each heaven its affair. And We adorned the nearest (lowest) heaven with lamps (stars) to be an adornment as well as to guard (from the devils by using them as missiles against them). Such is the decree of Him the All-Mighty,

the All-Knower.''[1]

He also says,

﴿أَوَلَمْ يَرَ ٱلَّذِينَ كَفَرُوٓاْ أَنَّ ٱلسَّمَوَٰتِ وَٱلْأَرْضَ كَانَتَا رَتْقًا فَفَتَقْنَٰهُمَا وَجَعَلْنَا مِنَ ٱلْمَآءِ كُلَّ شَيْءٍ حَيٍّ أَفَلَا يُؤْمِنُونَ ○ وَجَعَلْنَا فِي ٱلْأَرْضِ رَوَٰسِيَ أَن تَمِيدَ بِهِمْ وَجَعَلْنَا فِيهَا فِجَاجًا سُبُلًا لَّعَلَّهُمْ يَهْتَدُونَ ○ وَجَعَلْنَا ٱلسَّمَآءَ سَقْفًا مَّحْفُوظًا وَهُمْ عَنْ ءَايَٰتِهَا مُعْرِضُونَ﴾

"Have not those who disbelieve know that the heavens and the earth were joined together as one united piece, then We parted them? And We have made from water every living thing. Will they not then believe? And We have placed on the earth firm mountains, lest it should shake with them, and We placed therein broad highways for them to pass through, that they may be guided. And We have made heaven a roof, safe and well-guarded. Yet, they turn away from its signs.''[2]

Allâh created the universe for many great purposes. There are in every part of it great wisdom and dazzling signs. If you ponder over a single sign thereof, you will see wonders. Behold the wonders of the creation of Allâh in the plants in which almost every leaf, stem and fruit is full of benefit that human intellect cannot fully comprehend and understand its details. Behold the water courses of those tender and weak stems, which eyes can hardly see except by careful observation, how they are able to draw water from the bottom to the top and the water then moves in those courses according to their acceptability and capacities. It then breaks into particles that cannot be

---

[1] Fussilat 41:9-12
[2] Al-Anbiyâ' 21:30-32

perceived by human eyes. Then behold, the fruit of a tree and how it moves from a stage to another like the invincible movement of the conditions of a foetus. You see a tree growing from a mere naked wood with no covering on it, then its Lord and Creator covers it with leaves in the most beautiful manner. He then brings out its fruit tender and weak after He has brought out its leaf in order to preserve it and make it like a clothing for that weak fruit so as to protect it against heat, cold and other harmful phenomena. He then provides sustenance for these fruits through their stems and water courses so that they can be nourished by that, as an infant is nourished by the milk of its mother. He then nurtures the fruits and develop them until they become completely ripe. He thereby brought out that delicious fruit out of that lifeless wooden-like particle.

When you look at the earth and how it was created, you will see that it is one of the greatest signs of its Creator. Allâh makes it a resting place and as a bed, and subjected it to His slaves. He makes their sustenance, provision and sources of livelihood there and created therein for them ways and paths so that they can move about to meet their needs. He fixed it firmly with mountains and makes them as pillars in order to protect it against shaking. He flattens it, extends it and spreads it, makes it a receptacle for the living that brings them together on its surface and makes it a receptacle for the dead that bring them together in its interior after their death. Its surface is a place of dwelling for the living and its interior is the place of abode for the dead.

Then look at its revolving orbit, with its sun, moon, stars and zodiacs and behold how it continuously revolves around this world till the end of time in this order and proper succession and see the differences in the night, day, seasons, heat and cold which are results of these wonderful movements; and the benefits they give to all kinds of animals and plants and all that exists on the earth.

Then reflect over the creation of the heaven and take another look at it; you will see that it is one of the greatest signs of Allâh in altitude, expansiveness and stability. There is no pillar underneath it and there is no suspender over it but held by the infinite power of Allâh which holds the heaven and the earth lest they fall asunder.

When you also look at this universe, the composition of its parts and its best arrangement - that show the perfect omnipotence of their Creator and His perfect knowledge, wisdom and grace - you will find that it is like a constructed edifice in which all its tools and requirements are provided. The heaven was erected with its roof raised above it; the earth made like a place of rest and a carpet for its dwellers; the sun and moon which are like lamps illuminate the earth; and the stars which are its lanterns and adornment give directions to the traveller in the paths of the universe. The jewels and minerals that are hidden in the earth like prepared treasures are all made for the purpose that best suits them. All kinds of plants and animals are also prepared for what they are good for. Some animals are good for riding, some are good for milking; some are good for food and some are better used as guards. And He made man their controller and like an authorised king above all of them.

If you also ponder over this universe either in every respect or in a part of it, you will see a lot of wonders. If you deeply reflect and you are sincere with yourself and free yourself from the noose of whims and caprices and blind imitation, you will know with certainty that this universe was created by the All-Wise, All-Powerful and All-Knower, Who measured it in the best manner and arranged it in the best form. You will also know with certainty that it is simply impossible that the Creator should be two; He is only One Lord beside Whom there is none other worthy of worship and that had there been any other god in the heavens and the earth, their affairs would have been corrupted, their order disrupted and their welfare broken down.

If you however insist on attributing the creation to others beside the Creator, what will you say of the mechanism that revolves around a river whose tools and composition have been perfected and excellently measured that the looker does not see any defect in it or its picture. This river is situated in the middle of a long garden in which there are different kinds of fruits that get their water from this river; and there is in this garden a caretaker who brings its disunited parts together and perfectly takes care of it so that nothing of it becomes defected and nothing of its fruits becomes decayed. This caretaker then portions out its parts to the outlets according to man's needs and necessities, giving each group what it deserves and portioning it out in this way continuously.

Will you then say that all this happened without the hand of any creator, who has freedom of choice and is a planner? Will you say that the existence of that mechanism and garden is just accidental without any creator or planner? Can you imagine what your reason will tell you if all these were to come to being accidentally? Can you imagine as to where your reason will direct you and counsel you about?[1]

The Underlying Reasons

After all these reflections over the creation of the universe, we deem it fit to mention some of the reasons for which Allâh created these huge beings and astounding signs.

1. To subject them for man: When Allâh decreed to create a successor on this earth that would be worshipping him and inhabit the earth; He created all these things for him, that he might have an upright life and have his affairs of this life and that of his final abode put right for him. Allâh says,

$$﴿وَسَخَّرَ لَكُم مَّا فِى ٱلسَّمَٰوَٰتِ وَمَا فِى ٱلْأَرْضِ جَمِيعًا مِّنْهُ﴾$$

"And He subjected to you all that is in the heavens and all that is in the earth; it is all as a favour and kindness from Him."[2]

He also says,

$$﴿ٱللَّهُ ٱلَّذِى خَلَقَ ٱلسَّمَٰوَٰتِ وَٱلْأَرْضَ وَأَنزَلَ مِنَ ٱلسَّمَآءِ مَآءً$$

---

[1] This section is expunged from different places from the book, *"Miftaahu Daaris-sa 'aadat*, p 251-269.

[2] Al-Jâthiyah 45:13

فَأَخْرَجَ بِهِۦ مِنَ ٱلثَّمَرَٰتِ رِزْقًا لَّكُمْ وَسَخَّرَ لَكُمُ ٱلْفُلْكَ لِتَجْرِيَ فِى
ٱلْبَحْرِ بِأَمْرِهِۦ وَسَخَّرَ لَكُمُ ٱلْأَنْهَٰرَ ٥ وَسَخَّرَ لَكُمُ ٱلشَّمْسَ وَٱلْقَمَرَ
دَآئِبَيْنِ وَسَخَّرَ لَكُمُ ٱلَّيْلَ وَٱلنَّهَارَ ٥ وَءَاتَىٰكُم مِّن كُلِّ مَا سَأَلْتُمُوهُ
وَإِن تَعُدُّواْ نِعْمَتَ ٱللَّهِ لَا تُحْصُوهَآ إِنَّ ٱلْإِنسَٰنَ لَظَلُومٌ كَفَّارٌ ۞

*"Allâh is He Who has created the heavens and the
earth and sends down water (rain) from the sky, and
thereby brought forth fruits as provisions for you; and
He has made the ships to be of service to you, that they
may sail through the sea by His Command; and He
has made rivers (also) to be of service to you. And He
has made sun and moon, both constantly pursuing
their courses, to be of service to you; and He has made
the night and the day, to be of service to you. And He
gave you all of that you asked for, and if you count the
Blessings of Allâh, never will you be able to count
them. Verily, man is indeed an extreme wrong-doer, a
disbeliever."[1]*

2. To make the heavens and the earth and all that is in
    the universe proofs of Allâh's Lordship and signs of
    His Oneness. Because, the greatest thing in this life,
    is to affirm the Lordship of Allâh and His Oneness.
    And because of the fact that, it is the greatest
    matter, Allâh has established in its support greatest
    evidences and signs and proved it with the most
    convincing proofs. So, Allâh created the heavens,
    the earth and all other beings to make them
    evidences for that. That is why statements like,
    "Among His Signs" are mentioned in the abun-
    dance like in the following Verses.

---

[1] Ibrâhîm 14:32-34

﴿وَمِنْ ءَايَتِهِۦ خَلْقُ ٱلسَّمَوَتِ وَٱلْأَرْضِ﴾

"And among His Signs is the creation of the heavens and the earth."

﴿وَمِنْ ءَايَتِهِۦ مَنَامُكُم بِٱلَّيْلِ وَٱلنَّهَارِ﴾

"And among His Signs is the sleep that you take by night and by day."

﴿وَمِنْ ءَايَتِهِۦ يُرِيكُمُ ٱلْبَرْقَ خَوْفًا وَطَمَعًا﴾

"And among His Signs is that He shows you the lightning, by way of fear and hope."

﴿وَمِنْ ءَايَتِهِۦ أَن تَقُومَ ٱلسَّمَاءُ وَٱلْأَرْضُ بِأَمْرِهِۦ﴾

"And among His Signs is that the heavens and the earth stand by His Command."[1]

3. To make them evidences of the existence of the Day of Resurrection; since the life is two lives, a life of this world and a life of the Hereafter and the life of the Hereafter is the real life. Allâh says,

﴿وَمَا هَذِهِ ٱلْحَيَوٰةُ ٱلدُّنْيَا إِلَّا لَهْوٌ وَلَعِبٌ وَإِنَّ ٱلدَّارَ ٱلْأَخِرَةَ لَهِىَ ٱلْحَيَوَانُ لَوْ كَانُوا يَعْلَمُونَ﴾

"And this life of the world is only amusement and play! Verily, the home of the Hereafter - that is the life indeed (i.e., the eternal life that will never end), if they but knew."[2]

---

[1] Ar-Rûm 30:22-25

[2] Al-Ankabût 29:64

This is because the home of the Hereafter is the home of recompense and reckoning and there is the eternal bliss for those who deserve it and eternal torment for those who deserve it. Since man cannot reach that home except after he dies and is resurrected; its existence is denied by those whose relationship with their Lord has been cut, whose nature has suffered a relapse and whose sense of reasoning has been damaged. It is because of this that Allâh established proofs and evidences in order that souls might believe and hearts might have conviction; for reproduction of the soul is much easier than its first creation and the creation of the heavens and the earth is greater than the reproduction of man. Allâh says,

$$﴿وَهُوَ ٱلَّذِى يَبْدَؤُا۟ ٱلْخَلْقَ ثُمَّ يُعِيدُهُۥ وَهُوَ أَهْوَنُ عَلَيْهِ﴾$$

"And He it is Who originates the creation, then will repeat it (after it has been perished) and this is easier for Him."[1]

He also says,

$$﴿لَخَلْقُ ٱلسَّمَٰوَٰتِ وَٱلْأَرْضِ أَكْبَرُ مِنْ خَلْقِ ٱلنَّاسِ وَلَٰكِنَّ أَكْثَرَ ٱلنَّاسِ لَا يَعْلَمُونَ﴾$$

"The creation of the heavens and the earth is indeed greater than the creation of mankind, yet most of mankind know not."[2]

He also says,

---

[1] Ar-Rûm 30:27

[2] Ghâfir 40:57

﴿اللَّهُ الَّذِى رَفَعَ السَّمَوَاتِ بِغَيْرِ عَمَدٍ تَرَوْنَهَا ثُمَّ اسْتَوَىٰ عَلَى الْعَرْشِ وَسَخَّرَ الشَّمْسَ وَالْقَمَرَ كُلٌّ يَجْرِى لِأَجَلٍ مُّسَمًّى يُدَبِّرُ الْأَمْرَ يُفَصِّلُ الْآيَتِ لَعَلَّكُم بِلِقَاءِ رَبِّكُمْ تُوقِنُونَ﴾

"Allâh is He Who raised the heavens without any pillars that you can see. Then, He rose above the Throne (really in a manner that suits His Majesty). He has subjected the sun and the moon (to continue going round)! Each running (its course) for a time appointed. He regulates all affairs, explaining the proofs in detail, that you may believe with certainty in the meeting with your Lord."[1]

After all this O man! If all this universe has been subjected to you and all its signs and proofs have been shown to you, you will testify that there is no Lord worthy of worship except Allâh Alone Who has no partner. When you have known that your resurrection and life after death is easier than the creation of the heavens and the earth, that you shall meet your Lord Who will call you to account for your deeds and you have known that all this universe worships its Lord that all His creatures glorify their Lord with praises as confirmed by Allâh,

﴿يُسَبِّحُ لِلَّهِ مَا فِى السَّمَوَاتِ وَمَا فِى الْأَرْضِ الْمَلِكِ الْقُدُّوسِ الْعَزِيزِ الْحَكِيمِ﴾

"Whatsoever is in the heavens and whatsoever is in the earth glorifies Allâh, the King (of everything), the Holy, the All-Mighty, the All-Wise."[2]

---

[1] Ar-Ra'd 13:2
[2] Al-Jumu'ah 62:1

That, they all prostrate for His Majesty as He says,

﴿أَلَمْ تَرَ أَنَّ ٱللَّهَ يَسْجُدُ لَهُۥ مَن فِى ٱلسَّمَـٰوَٰتِ وَمَن فِى ٱلْأَرْضِ وَٱلشَّمْسُ وَٱلْقَمَرُ وَٱلنُّجُومُ وَٱلْجِبَالُ وَٱلشَّجَرُ وَٱلدَّوَآبُّ وَكَثِيرٌ مِّنَ ٱلنَّاسِ وَكَثِيرٌ حَقَّ عَلَيْهِ ٱلْعَذَابُ وَمَن يُهِنِ ٱللَّهُ فَمَا لَهُۥ مِن مُّكْرِمٍ إِنَّ ٱللَّهَ يَفْعَلُ مَا يَشَآءُ﴾

"See you not that to Allâh prostrates whoever is in the heavens and whoever is on the earth, and the sun, and the moon and the stars, and the mountains, and the trees, and the moving living creatures and many of mankind? But there are many (men) on whom the punishment is justified. And whomsoever Allâh disgraces none can honour him. Verily, Allâh does what He wills."[1]

Even these beings worship their Lord in a way that suits them as explained by Allâh in this verse,

﴿أَلَمْ تَرَ أَنَّ ٱللَّهَ يُسَبِّحُ لَهُۥ مَن فِى ٱلسَّمَـٰوَٰتِ وَٱلْأَرْضِ وَٱلطَّيْرُ صَآفَّـٰتٍ كُلٌّ قَدْ عَلِمَ صَلَاتَهُۥ وَتَسْبِيحَهُۥ﴾

"See you not that Allâh, He it is Whom glorify whatsoever is in the heavens and the earth, and the birds with wings out-spread (in flight). Of each one He knows indeed his prayer and his glorification [for every one knows his prayer and his glorification]."[2]

If your whole body does actually work in order according to the decree of Allâh and His regulation: the heart, the lungs, the liver and all other parts of the body submit and surrender to their Lord... Will your

---

[1] Al-Hajj 22:18
[2] An-Noor 24:41

optional decision after all this be between belief in your Lord and disbelief in Him? Will your decision be antipathy towards and deviation from this blessed path of the world around you and even of your body?

Actually, the completely sane man will consider himself far above choosing antipathy and deviation in the vastness of this great universe.

Creating and Honouring Man

It was a decision of Allâh to create a creature that could inhabit this universe and His choice fell on man. It is also in accordance with His Divine Wisdom that the matter from which man was created was the earth. He originated his creation from clay and then moulded him on this beautiful shape that he has now. When he has become completely perfect in that shape, He breathed life into him through His Spirit (Angel Jibreel - Gabriel) and He made him become man in the best form; provided him with the ability to hear, see, move and speak. Then his Lord made him live in Paradise, taught him all that he needed to know, made lawful for him all that was in Paradise and forbade him from a single tree - as a test for him.

Allâh wanted to show man's position and standing; so He commanded His Angels to prostrate for him. All of the Angels prostrated but Satan arrogantly and obstinately refused to prostrate. So Allâh became angry with him for his disobedience and expelled him from His Mercy because of his arrogance. Satan asked Allâh to extend his life and give him respite till the Day of Resurrection. So, Allâh extended his life till the Day of Resurrection.

Satan became envious of Adam because of the preference he and his children were given over him. He swore by His Lord that he would mislead all the children of Adam, that he would come to them from their front and rear, and from their left and from their right except the sincere, pious and truthful slaves of

Allâh among them, for such Allâh has protected against the evil plans of Satan. Allâh warned Adam of the evil plan of Satan, but Satan tempted Adam and his wife Hawwa in order to get them out of Paradise and to uncover for them that which was hidden from them of their private parts. He swore by Allâh to them that he was a sincere well-wisher for them and that Allâh had not forbidden them from that tree save they should become angels or become of the immortals.

Having been influenced by the deception of Satan, Adam and Hawwa ate of the forbidden tree and the first punishment that afflicted them for their disobedience of Allâh's command was that, which that was hidden from them of their private parts became exposed and Allâh reminded them of His warning about the tricks of Satan.

Adam then sought for the forgiveness of his Lord. So Allâh forgave Him, accepted his repentance, chose him and guided him. He then ordered him to descend from the Paradise where he was living, to the earth wherein there was his abode and his enjoyment for a time. He also told him that it was from earth that he was created, that on it he would live and die and that it is from it that he would be resurrected.

Adam and his wife Hawwa then descended to the earth and their children procreated and they all used to worship Allâh, because their father Adam was a Prophet. Allâh tells us this story in the glorious Qur'ân where He says,

$$﴿وَلَقَدْ خَلَقْنَٰكُمْ ثُمَّ صَوَّرْنَٰكُمْ ثُمَّ قُلْنَا لِلْمَلَٰٓئِكَةِ ٱسْجُدُوا۟ لِءَادَمَ$$

فَسَجَدُوٓاْ إِلَّآ إِبْلِيسَ لَمْ يَكُن مِّنَ ٱلسَّـٰجِدِينَ ○ قَالَ مَا مَنَعَكَ أَلَّا تَسْجُدَ
إِذْ أَمَرْتُكَ قَالَ أَنَا۠ خَيْرٌ مِّنْهُ خَلَقْتَنِى مِن نَّارٍ وَخَلَقْتَهُۥ مِن طِينٍ ○ قَالَ فَٱهْبِطْ
مِنْهَا فَمَا يَكُونُ لَكَ أَن تَتَكَبَّرَ فِيهَا فَٱخْرُجْ إِنَّكَ مِنَ ٱلصَّـٰغِرِينَ ○ قَالَ أَنظِرْنِى
إِلَىٰ يَوْمِ يُبْعَثُونَ ○ قَالَ إِنَّكَ مِنَ ٱلْمُنظَرِينَ ﴾

"And surely We created you (your father Adam) and then gave you shape, then We told the angels, 'Prostrate to Adam', and they prostrated except Iblees (Satan), he refused to be of those who prostrate. (Allâh) said, 'What prevented you (O Iblees) that you did not prostrate when I commanded you?' Iblees said, 'I am better than him (Adam), You created me from fire and You created him from clay.' Allâh said, '(O Iblees) get down from this (Paradise), it is not for you to be arrogant here. Get out, for you are of those humiliated and disgraced.' (Iblees) said, 'Allow me respite till the Day they are raised up.' Allâh said, 'You are of those allowed respite...' "[1]

﴿ فَتَبَارَكَ ٱللَّهُ أَحْسَنُ ٱلْخَـٰلِقِينَ ﴾

"So blessed is Allâh, the Best of creators."[2]

Consider the greatness of Allâh's work in man. He created him in the best form, clothed him with traits of honour like intellect, knowledge, eloquence, art of speaking, beautiful figure, moderate body, ability to acquire knowledge through analogical deduction and thinking and ability to acquire noble characteristics like, righteousness, acts of obedience and submission

[1] Al- A'raaf 7:11-15
[2] Al-Mu'minoon 23:14

to Allâh. Far is his condition while he was just a drop
of sperm kept in the womb of his mother from his
creation while the Angel will enter upon him in the
Paradise.

This world is a village and man is its inhabitant. All is
preoccupied because of him and all is made to work
for his interests. All other creatures are made to serve
him and provide for his needs. The angels are charged
to protect him during day and night. Those of them
who are charged with provision of rain and plants
strive to provide him with his sustenance; orbits are
made to surrender to him and revolve in his services;
the sun, moon and stars are all subjected to move in
line with his time reckoning and for the betterment of
his food arrangement. The aerial world with its winds,
clouds, birds and all that it contains is also subjected to
him. So is the lower world with all its seas and rivers,
its trees and fruits, its plants and animals and all that is
in it. Allâh says,

$$﴿ٱللَّهُ ٱلَّذِى خَلَقَ ٱلسَّمَٰوَٰتِ وَٱلْأَرْضَ وَأَنزَلَ مِنَ ٱلسَّمَآءِ مَآءً$$
$$فَأَخْرَجَ بِهِۦ مِنَ ٱلثَّمَرَٰتِ رِزْقًا لَّكُمْ وَسَخَّرَ لَكُمُ ٱلْفُلْكَ لِتَجْرِىَ فِى$$
$$ٱلْبَحْرِ بِأَمْرِهِۦ وَسَخَّرَ لَكُمُ ٱلْأَنْهَٰرَ ٠ وَسَخَّرَ لَكُمُ ٱلشَّمْسَ وَٱلْقَمَرَ$$
$$دَآئِبَيْنِ وَسَخَّرَ لَكُمُ ٱلَّيْلَ وَٱلنَّهَارَ ٠ وَءَاتَىٰكُم مِّن كُلِّ مَا سَأَلْتُمُوهُ$$
$$وَإِن تَعُدُّواْ نِعْمَتَ ٱللَّهِ لَا تُحْصُوهَآ إِنَّ ٱلْإِنسَٰنَ لَظَلُومٌ كَفَّارٌ ﴾$$

*"Allâh is He Who has created the heavens and the
earth and sends down water (rain) from the sky, and
thereby brought forth fruits as provisions for you; and
he has made the ship to be of service to you, that may
sail through the sea by His Command; and He has
made rivers also to be of service to you. And He has*

made the sun and the moon, both constantly pursuing their courses, to be of service to you; and He has made the night and the day, to be of service to you. And He gave you all that you asked for, and if you count the blessings of Allâh, never will you be able to reckon them. Verily, man is indeed an extreme wrong-doer, a disbeliever.''[1]

To complete His honour on man, He created for him all that he needs in his worldly life and all that he needs that can make him attain the highest positions in the Hereafter. He as such, revealed to him His Books and sent to him His Messengers explaining to him the Law of Allâh and calling him unto it.

Then Allâh created for him from his own self - meaning from Adam himself - a wife, so that he might enjoy the pleasure of living with her, in response to his natural needs, be it psychological, intellectual and physical. He then found with her comfort, tranquillity and stability and both of them found in their togetherness peace, contentedness, love and mercy; because of their physical, psychological and nervous composition, both of them are made to respond to the desires of each other and both are made to be in harmony in the process of producing new generations. The souls of both are enriched with these feelings and their relationship is filled with comfort for the soul and nerves, peace for the body and mind, stability for the life and subsistence, familiarity for souls and conscience and a tranquillity for the man and woman on an equal basis.

---

[1] Ibrâhîm 14:32-34

Allâh then chose the believers among mankind and made them his friends. He made them obey Him and work for Him according to his Laws in order to make them qualify to live in His Paradise. He chose among them Prophets, Messengers, saints and martyrs and blessed them in this world with the best favour that human souls can enjoy: worshipping Allâh, obeying Him and supplicating to Him. He also distinguished them with great favours - that others cannot get - among which are: peace, tranquillity and happiness, and greater than all this is the fact that they know the truth that was brought by the Messengers and believe in it. Allâh then keeps for them - in the Hereafter - the everlasting bliss and great success that befit His generosity, glory be to Him. He will also reward their belief in Him and their sincerity to Him and will give them more out of His Bounty.

The position of woman:

In Islâm, the woman is accorded a high position which she was not accorded in any of the previous religions and which no nation will accord her but Islâm. This is because, the honour that Islâm conferred on mankind is shared by both man and woman on equal basis. Mankind are equal before rules of Allâh in this world as they will be equal as regards His reward and recompense on the Last Day. Allâh says,

$$﴿وَلَقَدْ كَرَّمْنَا بَنِيٓ ءَادَمَ﴾$$

"And indeed, We have honoured the children of Adam."[1]

---
[1] Al-Isrâ' 17:70.

He also says,

﴿لِّلرِّجَالِ نَصِيبٌ مِّمَّا تَرَكَ ٱلْوَٰلِدَانِ وَٱلْأَقْرَبُونَ﴾

"There is a share for men and a share for women from what is left by parents and those nearest related."[1]

﴿وَلَهُنَّ مِثْلُ ٱلَّذِى عَلَيْهِنَّ بِٱلْمَعْرُوفِ﴾

"And they (women) have rights (over their husbands as regards living expenses) similar (to those of their husbands) over them (as regards obedience and respect) to what is reasonable."[2]

﴿وَٱلْمُؤْمِنُونَ وَٱلْمُؤْمِنَٰتُ بَعْضُهُمْ أَوْلِيَآءُ بَعْضٍ﴾

"The believers, men and women are auliya (helpers, supporters, friends, protectors) of one another."[3]

﴿وَقَضَىٰ رَبُّكَ أَلَّا تَعْبُدُوٓا۟ إِلَّآ إِيَّاهُ وَبِٱلْوَٰلِدَيْنِ إِحْسَٰنًا ۚ إِمَّا يَبْلُغَنَّ عِندَكَ ٱلْكِبَرَ أَحَدُهُمَآ أَوْ كِلَاهُمَا فَلَا تَقُل لَّهُمَآ أُفٍّ وَلَا تَنْهَرْهُمَا وَقُل لَّهُمَا قَوْلًا كَرِيمًا ۝ وَٱخْفِضْ لَهُمَا جَنَاحَ ٱلذُّلِّ مِنَ ٱلرَّحْمَةِ وَقُل رَّبِّ ٱرْحَمْهُمَا كَمَا رَبَّيَانِى صَغِيرًا ۝﴾

"And your Lord has decreed that you worship none but Him. And that you be dutiful to your parents. If one of them or both of them attain old age in your life, say not to them a word of disrespect, nor shout at them but address them in terms of honour. And lower unto them a wing of submission and humility through mercy, and say; 'My Lord! Bestow on them Your

---

[1] An-Nisâ' 4: 7

[2] Al-Baqarah 2: 228

[3] At-Tawbah 9:71

Mercy as they did bring me up when I was young.'[1]

﴿فَٱسْتَجَابَ لَهُمْ رَبُّهُمْ أَنِّى لَا أُضِيعُ عَمَلَ عَٰمِلٍ مِّنكُم مِّن ذَكَرٍ أَوْ أُنثَىٰ﴾

"So their Lord accepted their supplication (saying); 'Never will I allow to be lost the work of any of you, be he male or female.'[2]

﴿مَنْ عَمِلَ صَٰلِحًا مِّن ذَكَرٍ أَوْ أُنثَىٰ وَهُوَ مُؤْمِنٌ فَلَنُحْيِيَنَّهُ حَيَوٰةً طَيِّبَةً وَلَنَجْزِيَنَّهُمْ أَجْرَهُم بِأَحْسَنِ مَا كَانُوا۟ يَعْمَلُونَ﴾

"Whoever works righteousness - whether male or female - while he or she is a true believer (of Islâmic monotheism) verily, to him We will give a good life (in this world with respect, contentment and lawful provision), and We shall pay them certainly a reward in proportion to the best of what they used to do.'[3]

﴿وَمَن يَعْمَلْ مِنَ ٱلصَّٰلِحَٰتِ مِن ذَكَرٍ أَوْ أُنثَىٰ وَهُوَ مُؤْمِنٌ فَأُو۟لَٰئِكَ يَدْخُلُونَ ٱلْجَنَّةَ وَلَا يُظْلَمُونَ نَقِيرًا﴾

'And whoever does righteous good deeds, male or female, and is a true believer (in the Oneness of Allâh), such will enter paradise and not the least injustice, even to the size of a speck on the back of a date-stone, will be done to them.'[4]

This honour that the woman enjoys in Islâm has no equal in any other religion, creed or law. Roman civilization had had it established that woman should

---

[1] Al-Isrâ' 17: 23-24.
[2] Al-Imrân 3:195
[3] An-Nahl 16: 97
[4] An-Nisâ' 4: 124

be a slave and a subordinate of man and that she should absolutely has no rights at all. There was even a great conference in Rome where affairs of the woman were discussed. The conclusion reached at the conference was that, the woman was a lifeless being and as such could not have share in the life of the Hereafter and that she was impure.

In Athens, woman used to be regarded as a scraps. She would be sold and bought like any other commodity and she was being regarded an abomination of Satan's handiwork.

According to the ancient Indian statutes, the plague, death, hell, poison of serpents and fire are all better than woman. Her right to live used to end with the death of her husband - who was regarded as her master. When she saw the corpse of her husband being burnt, she must throw herself into it and if she did not, she would be accursed.

As for Judaism, the following judgement was passed on her in the Old Testament.

"I moved around with my heart in order to know, search and look for wisdom and intelligence, and in other to know that evil is ignorance and that stupidity is madness. And I found that worse than death is woman who is a snare and her heart is like a shoelace and her hands are shackles."[1]

---

[1] *Sifrul jaami 'ah* 7:25-26. It is known that the Old Testament is hallowed and believed in by both the Christians and the Jews. Note: The two verses were translated directly from Arabic version quoted by the author because the translator could not find them in the Biblical version available to him nor could he find the name of the book in English.=Translator.

Such was the condition of woman in the ancient times. As for medieval and contemporary times, the following events explain that.

The Danish writer, Wieth Kordsten explained the position of the Catholic Church as regards woman when he said, "During the medieval times, the concern that was had for European woman was very limited and this is in conformity with the view of the Catholic creed that used to regard woman as a second-class human being."

In France, a conference was held in the year 586 A.D. where the issue of woman was discussed as to whether she should be regarded as a human being or not. At the end of the discussion, the discussants concluded that she was a human being but that she was created for the service of man.

In French law, article 217 says; "The married woman-even if her marriage is based on separation between her right of ownership and that of her husband-should not give anyone ownership of anything of her property with or without compensation except with the participation of her husband in the transaction or his written consent to that."

In England, Henry the VIII prohibited the English woman from reading the Holy Book, until 1850, women were not considered citizens of England and up till 1882, they had no personal rights.[1]

As for the condition of woman in contemporary

---

[1] *Silsilatu Muqaaranatil Adyaan* — Dr. Ahmad Shalaby 3/210-213.

Europe, America and other industrial nations, she is regarded as a common creature that should be utilized for commercial purposes, for she is a part of commercial advertisement. This has even reached a situation where she is stripped naked in order to advertise commodities on her body. Her body and honour have become desecrated based on regulations laid down by men in order to make her an object of enjoyment everywhere.

The contemporary woman is an abject of care and attention as long as she is able to give out her wealth, intelligence and body. But when she becomes old and loses her means of giving, the society individually and collectively abandons her and she lives lonely in her house or in the sanatorium.

Compare the above - although they cannot be equal - with what the Noble Qur'ân says,

﴿وَٱلْمُؤْمِنُونَ وَٱلْمُؤْمِنَٰتُ بَعْضُهُمْ أَوْلِيَآءُ بَعْضٍ﴾

"The believers men and women are friends of one another."[1]

﴿وَلَهُنَّ مِثْلُ ٱلَّذِى عَلَيْهِنَّ بِٱلْمَعْرُوفِ﴾

"And they (women) have rights (over their husbands) similar (to those of their husbands) over them."[2]

﴿وَقَضَىٰ رَبُّكَ أَلَّا تَعْبُدُوٓا۟ إِلَّآ إِيَّاهُ وَبِٱلْوَٰلِدَيْنِ إِحْسَٰنًا إِمَّا يَبْلُغَنَّ عِندَكَ ٱلْكِبَرَ أَحَدُهُمَآ أَوْ كِلَاهُمَا فَلَا تَقُل لَّهُمَآ أُفٍّ وَلَا تَنْهَرْهُمَا وَقُل﴾

[1] At-Tawbah 9: 71

[2] Al-Baqarah 2: 228

لَّهُمَا قَوْلًا كَرِيمًا ○ وَٱخْفِضْ لَهُمَا جَنَاحَ ٱلذُّلِّ مِنَ ٱلرَّحْمَةِ وَقُل رَّبِّ ٱرْحَمْهُمَا كَمَا رَبَّيَانِي صَغِيرًا ﴿

"And your Lord has decreed that you worship none but Him. And that you be dutiful to your parents. If one of them or both of them attain old age in your life, say not to them a word of disrespect, nor shout at them but address them in terms of honour. And lower unto them the wing of submission and humility through mercy, and say: 'My Lord! Bestow on them your mercy as they did bring me up when I was young.'[1]

While Allâh honours woman, He makes it clear to all mankind that He created her to be mother, wife, daughter and sister; and ordained for these roles, special regulations that are peculiar to her.

---

[1] Al-Isrâ' 17: 23-24

Why Was Man Created?

It has been discussed in the previous chapter that, Allâh created Adam and created for him his wife, Hawwa and made them live in Paradise. Then Adam disobeyed his Lord and later sought for His forgiveness. Allâh then accepted his repentance and guided him. Allâh then ordered him to go out of the Paradise and descend unto the earth. Allâh, glory be to Him and He be exalted has in that, a wisdom which human intelligence can not perceive and which their tongue can not describe. We are going to mention here some of those wisdoms and underlying reasons.

1. That Allâh created the creation for His worship. That is the purpose of creating them. He says,

$$﴿وَمَا خَلَقْتُ ٱلْجِنَّ وَٱلْإِنسَ إِلَّا لِيَعْبُدُونِ﴾$$

"And I created not the jinn and mankind except that they should worship Me." [1]

It is also known that the perfection of the worship that is required of man can not take in the abode of bliss and eternity but in the abode of trials and tribulation. The abode of eternity is that of bliss, not that of examination and commandments.

2. Allâh wanted to take among mankind Prophets, Messengers, friends and martyrs whom He would love and who would love Him. He then left them alone with his enemies and put them to trial by

---
[1] Adh-Dhâriyât 51: 56

them. So when they preferred Him above all other things and sacrificed their lives and properties in order to gain His pleasure and love, they attained of His love and pleasure what they could not have attained without that initially. So the status of prophethood and martyrdom is of the best degrees before Allâh and could not have attained that except by the way decreed by Allâh that Adam and his offspring had to descend to the earth.

3. Allâh is the only True and Evident King. The King is the One Who commands and forbids; rewards and punishes; disgraces and honours; strengthens and debases. Allâh's sovereignty therefore necessitates that He sends Adam and his offspring to an abode in which the rules of sovereignty will be implemented on them and then move them to an abode where there is reward for all that they did.

4. Allâh created Adam from a handful of all soils of the earth; and there is good and bad and low and high in the land. Allâh knows that there are among - the children of Adam - those who are unsuitable to stay with Him in His house, therefore, He made Adam descend to an abode where He distinguishes between the good and bad ones. Then Allâh chose for them two distinct abodes: He made good ones dwellers of His Abode (made them enter Paradise), and made the bad ones dwellers of the abode of misery (Hell-Fire).

5. To Allâh belong the Beautiful Names. Among His Names are: Al-Ghafoor (the Oft-Forgiving), Ar-Raheem (the Most-Gracious). Al-Afuww (Oft-Par-

doning), Al-Haleem (Most-Forbearing). Since the impacts of these names must manifest, the Wisdom of Allâh necessitates that Adam and his children must descend to an abode where the impacts of the Beautiful Names of Allâh could materialise on them. So that He might forgive whoever He wills, have mercy on whomever He wills, pardon whosoever He wills and forbear for whosoever He wills and other different ways in which His Names and Attributes can be manifest.

6. Allâh created Adam and his children from a composition that is naturally inclined to good and evil, responsive to the causes of lusts and temptations and to the causes of reason and knowledge. He created in him reason and lust and created in both necessary factors so that His Will might be accomplished and that He might show to His slaves His greatness in Wisdom, Might; and His Mercy, Kindness and Benevolence in His Authority and Sovereignty. He then, out of His Wisdom sent Adam and his children to the earth so that the test might take place therein and impacts of man's preparedness for these factors and his responsiveness to them might become manifest, and Allâh may then use that basis to award honour or disgrace to whom it is due.

7. Belief in the Unseen is the useful belief. As for the belief in the seen, everyone will believe on the Day of Resurrection. If people were created in the Abode of Bliss (Paradise), they would not have attained the degree of belief in the Unseen that ends in enjoyment and honour. It is for this reason that

Allâh sent them to the abode in which they could have opportunity to believe in the Unseen.

8. Allâh wants by that, to show His slaves on whom He has bestowed His favour, the perfection of that favour and its greatness so that they might thank Allâh and love Him the most and have the fullest enjoyment of the bliss which Allâh has bestowed on them. Allâh therefore, shows them what He did to His enemies and the punishment that He has prepared for them. He also makes them witness the highest kinds of bliss which He has bestowed on them, so that their joy might increase. This is an aspect of completing His favours on them. There- fore, to make them achieve all this, He must send them to the earth, put them to test and then make whosoever He wills to succeed out of mercy and kindness from Him, and disgrace whosoever He wills among them out of His wisdom and justice, for He is All-Knower, All-Wise.

9. Allâh wants Adam and his children to go back to the Paradise while they are in the best state. So before they enter it, He wants to make them taste of the hardship, sorrow and distress of the world so that the value of entering Paradise in the Hereafter will be great in their estimation, for it is the opposite of an object that shows its beauty.[1]

After the origin of man has been made clear, it is now appropriate to explain his need for the true religion.

---

[1] See: *Miftaah Daaris-Sa'aadah* 1 / 6-11

Man's Need for Religion

Man's need for religion is greater than his need for other necessities of life. For, man must know the things that please Allâh as well as those that displease Him. He must also carry out activities that can bring him benefits and others that can avert from him harm. So, it is the Divine Law that distinguishes between the deeds that benefit and those that bring harm. That is Allâh's justice in His creation and His Light among His servants and it is not possible for people to live without Divine Law with which they can differentiate between what they should do and what they should not do.

If man actually has a will, he must then know what he wants. Does he want what will benefit him or what will harm him? Does he want what will reform him or what will corrupt him? Some people know this naturally, some know it through application of their sense of reasoning and some yet do not know it except through explanation by the Messengers and their guidance.[1]

However the atheistic and materialistic thoughts may be widespread and adorned; and ideologies and theories thrive, individuals and societies will never do without true religion. For these ideologies can never provide for man's spiritual and physical needs. And the more man goes deeper in them, the more he is

---

[1] See *At-Tadmuriyyah by Sheikhul-Islâm Ibn Taymiyyah* p. 213-214; and *Miftaahu Daaris-Sa'aadah* 2 / 383.

convinced that they cannot give him security nor satiate his thirst and that the true religion is unavoidable.

Ernest Rinan said, "All things that we hold dear can dwindle, and freedom of using one's intelligence, knowledge and expertise can become worthless. But it is impossible for religion to be effaced. It will rather remain a living proof on the futility of material ideology that wants to restrict man into despicable narrows of the earthly life."[1]

Muhammad Fareed Wajdee said: "It is impossible for religious thinking to vanish, for it is the highest and noblest of human mind's inclinations, not to mention the fact that it is an inclination that elevates man. Rather than dwindle, this inclination shall be increasing. Religious nature of man will always pursue him as long as he can discern what is beautiful and what is ugly and this nature shall continue to increase in him according to sublimity of his mental faculties and progress in his knowledge."[2]

So if man keeps away from his Lord, it is through the sublimity of his mental faculties and wideness of his knowledge that he recognizes the greatness of his ignorance about his Lord and what is due to Him, and his ignorance of his own self, what is good for him and what is harmful to him; what gives him happiness and what will cause him misery. He will also recognise his ignorance of scientific details like astronomy, science

---

[1] See *Ad-Deen* by Muhammad Abdullah Daraaz p. 87.
[2] *Ibid.* 88.

of galaxies, reckoning, nuclear sciences and so forth. It is then that the world will abandon the stage of delusion and arrogance to that of humility and submission and then believe that there is behind these sciences a knowledgeable and Wise One and that there is behind the nature an Able Creator. This reality will then force the impartial scholar to believe in the unseen, to surrender to the upright religion and to respond to the call of natural instinct. But when man withdraws from this path, his nature will relapse and he will come down to the level of dumb animals.

We conclude from all the above, that the true religiosity - that depends on belief in the Oneness of Allâh and performing acts of worship according to His injunctions - is a necessary element of life, so that man actualizes through that, his servitude to Allâh, Lord of all the worlds and attain through that, happiness and safety from destruction, hardship and misery. It is also necessary for perfecting the theoretical aptitude in man. It is only through it that the intellectual hunger can be satiated, and its highest goals attained.

Equally, religion is a necessary element for purification of the soul and refinement of emotional power, for noble sentiments find in the religion an abundant space and a spring whose water does not dry up where noble sentiments find their goals attained.

It is a necessary element for the perfection of will power because of the support it gives it through great impetus and major means of resisting elements of despair.

In view of this, if there are some who say that man is

civil by nature, we must also say: "Man is religious by nature", for man has two powers: scientific speculative power and will power. His complete happiness depends on perfecting his scientific and will power and the perfection of his scientific power cannot take place except by knowing the following:

1. Knowing the True Lord Who is the Creator and the Provider; Who created man from nothingness and bestowed on him favours.

2. Knowing His Names and Attributes and all that is due to Him; and the impacts of these Names on His slaves.

3. Knowing the way that leads to Him, may He be glorified.

4. Knowing the hindrances and harms that prevent man from knowing the way and the great bliss that the way leads to.

5. Having a real cognisance of your own soul, its needs, recognising what is good for it and what is harm to it, and knowing its qualities and defects.

It is by knowing these five things that man can perfect his scientific power. And perfection of his scientific and will power can not occur except by respecting the rights of Allâh upon His slaves and carrying out these rights sincerely, truthfully, according to the *Sunnah* of the Prophet 鑑 and as a testimony of His favour on him. There is no way to perfection of these two powers except by His help. He therefore needs to be guided to the

Straight Path which Allâh guided His friends.[1]

After we have known that the True Religion is the Divine support for different powers of the soul, we should also know that religion is the protective shield for the society. This is because human life cannot be alright except through mutual cooperation and this cooperation cannot take place except through a system that regulates human relationships, defines their obligations and guarantees their rights. This system is also in need of a curbing and restraining authority that can prevent the soul from violating the system, encourage it to preserve it, guarantees its relevance and prevents men from desecrating it. What then is this power?

There is not on the face of this earth any power that can match the power of religiosity or even close to that in guaranteeing the respect for order, societal cohesion, stability of it's system and harmonising the means of comfort and tranquillity in the society.

The underlying reason for this is that, man is distinguished from other living things in that, all his voluntary movements and actions are controlled by an inaudible and invincible element. That element is faith which refines the soul and purifies the limbs. Man, is therefore, always controlled by a true or false belief. If his belief is correct, everything in him will be correct, but if his belief is corrupt, everything in him will be corrupt.

Faith is a spontaneous watcher over man; and it is - as noticed in all men - of two types:

---

[1] *Al-Fawaaid* 18,19.

- Belief in the value of moral excellence, human dignity and other ordinary concepts that high-minded people will feel shy to violate even if they were free from external consequences and material recompense.

- Belief in Allâh - may He be Glorified and Exalted - and the fact that He is Ever-Watchful of the secrets and knows all that is hidden; from Whose Commandments and prohibitions the Islâmic Law derives its power and before Whom the senses profusely feel mortified out of love for Him or fear of Him or both. There is no doubt that this type of faith is the stronger of both in exerting authority over human mind. It is also the stronger in resisting the tornadoes of whims and inconsistency of sentiments and quicker in leaving impacts on the minds of people and their leaders.

It is because of this that religion is the best guarantor for the establishment of relationships among people on the basis of justice and impartiality which is a necessity in any society. There is no wonder then that religion occupies in the human society the position of the heart in human body.[1]

If this is the position of religion generally - and what we see in today's world is multiplicity of religions and creeds, where each group rejoices in its belief and holds tenaciously to it - what then is the true religion that can achieve for the human mind what it yearns for? And what are the general criteria of the True Religion?

---

[1] See: Ad-deen p. 98, 102.

General Criteria of the True Religion

Every adherent of a creed believes that his creed is the true one, and all followers of a religion believe that their religion is the ideal one and the most upright path. When you ask the followers of adulterated religions or followers of man-made creeds about the proof for their belief, they argue that they found their fathers on a faith and are just following their paths. They then relate narrations and stories whose chains of transmitters are not sound and whose texts are not free from faults and defects. They only depend on inherited books whose authors, recorders and even their original languages and their sources are unknown. They are only mixed-up stories concocted together, magnified and inherited generation after generation without any scholastic verification of their chains of transmitters and precise checking of their texts.

These unknown books, narrations and blind imitations cannot be taken as evidences in matters of religions and beliefs. Or is it possible that all these adulterated religions and man-made creeds are true or false?

It is impossible that all these religions are true, for truth is only one and cannot be numerous. It is also impossible that all these adulterated religions and man-made beliefs are all from Allâh and therefore true. Then, since there are numerous religions and the true is only one, which of them is then the true religion? There should, therefore, be criteria for distinguishing the true religion from the false. If we find that these criteria fit a religion, we know that it is the true religion; and when all or one of these criteria is lacking in any religion, we know that it is a false religion.

The criteria by which we distinguish the true religion from the false ones are:

One: That the religion must be from Allâh, revealed through an angel to one of His Messengers in order to convey it to mankind. For the true religion is Allâh's, and it is He Who will recompense His slaves and take them to reckoning on the Day of Resurrection concerning the religion that He revealed to them. He says,

﴿إِنَّا أَوْحَيْنَا إِلَيْكَ كَمَا أَوْحَيْنَا إِلَىٰ نُوحٍ وَالنَّبِيِّنَ مِنۢ بَعْدِهِۦ وَأَوْحَيْنَا إِلَىٰ إِبْرَٰهِيمَ وَإِسْمَٰعِيلَ وَإِسْحَٰقَ وَيَعْقُوبَ وَالْأَسْبَاطِ وَعِيسَىٰ وَأَيُّوبَ وَيُونُسَ وَهَٰرُونَ وَسُلَيْمَٰنَ وَءَاتَيْنَا دَاوُۥدَ زَبُورًا﴾

"Verily, We have sent the revelation to you (O Muhammad ﷺ) as We sent the revelation to Nûh (Noah) and the Prophets after him; We also sent the revelation to Ibrahîm (Abraham), Ismaa'eel (Ishmael), Is'haaq (Issac), Ya'qoob (Jacob) and Al-Asbaat (the offspring of the twelve sons of Ya'qoob), 'Eesaa (Jesus), Ayoob (Job), Yûnus (Jonah), Haroon (Aaron) and Sulaiman (Solomon); and to Dawood (David) We gave the Psalms."[1]

He, may He be glorified- also says,

_____
[1] An-Nisâ' 4:163

﴿وَمَآ أَرْسَلْنَا مِن قَبْلِكَ مِن رَّسُولٍ إِلَّا نُوحِى إِلَيْهِ أَنَّهُ لَا إِلَهَ إِلَّا أَنَا۠ فَٱعْبُدُونِ﴾

"And We did not send any Messenger before you (O Muhammad) but We revealed to him (saying): none has the right to be worshipped but Me. So worship Me."[1]

Based on the above Verses and criteria, any religion that is brought by any man and attributed to himself and not to Allâh is definitely a false religion.

Two: That the religion should call to the worship of Allâh alone; should prohibit *Shirk* (polytheism of any form) and all that can lead to it. This is because, the call to the oneness of Allâh is the primary mission of all Prophets and Messengers. Every Prophet told his people:

﴿ٱعْبُدُوا۟ ٱللَّهَ مَا لَكُم مِّنْ إِلَهٍ غَيْرُهُۥٓ﴾

"Worship Allâh! You have no other god but Him."[2]

Three: It should be in agreement with the principles unto which all the Messengers call their people which are to worship Allâh alone and to avoid polytheism, unruliness to parents, killing of a person unjustly and all other immoral things, be they hidden or apparent. Allâh says,

﴿وَمَآ أَرْسَلْنَا مِن قَبْلِكَ مِن رَّسُولٍ إِلَّا نُوحِى إِلَيْهِ أَنَّهُ لَا إِلَهَ إِلَّا أَنَا۠ فَٱعْبُدُونِ﴾

---

[1] Al-Anbiyâ' 21:25

[2] Al-A'râf 7:73

"And We did not send any Messenger before you (O Muhammad) but We revealed to Him (saying): None has the right to be worshipped but I, so worship Me."[1]

He also says,

﴿قُل تَعَالَوْا أَتْلُ مَا حَرَّمَ رَبُّكُمْ عَلَيْكُمْ أَلَّا تُشْرِكُوا بِهِ شَيْئًا وَبِٱلْوَٰلِدَيْنِ إِحْسَٰنًا وَلَا تَقْتُلُوٓا أَوْلَٰدَكُم مِّنْ إِمْلَٰقٍ نَّحْنُ نَرْزُقُكُمْ وَإِيَّاهُمْ وَلَا تَقْرَبُوا ٱلْفَوَٰحِشَ مَا ظَهَرَ مِنْهَا وَمَا بَطَنَ وَلَا تَقْتُلُوا ٱلنَّفْسَ ٱلَّتِى حَرَّمَ ٱللَّهُ إِلَّا بِٱلْحَقِّ ذَٰلِكُمْ وَصَّىٰكُم بِهِۦ لَعَلَّكُمْ تَعْقِلُونَ﴾

"Say (O Muhammad): Come I will recite what your Lord has prohibited you from: Join not anything in worship with Him; be good and dutiful to your parents; kill not your children because of poverty - We provide sustenance for you and for them; come not near to Al-Fawaahish (Shameful sins, illegal sexual intercourse) whether committed openly or secretly; and kill not anyone whom Allâh has forbidden, except for a just cause (according to Islâmic Law). This He has commanded you that you may understand."[2]

He also says,

﴿وَسْـَٔلْ مَنْ أَرْسَلْنَا مِن قَبْلِكَ مِن رُّسُلِنَآ أَجَعَلْنَا مِن دُونِ ٱلرَّحْمَٰنِ ءَالِهَةً يُعْبَدُونَ﴾

"And ask (O Muhammad) those of Our Messengers whom We sent before you: 'Did We ever appoint gods

---
[1] Al-Anbiyâ' 21:25
[2] Al-An'âm 6:151

to be worshipped besides the Most-Gracious (Allâh)."[1]

Four: It should not be self-contradicting by commanding a matter and contradicting it by another. It should also not forbid something and then allow what is similar to it without any reason or prohibit something for some group and permit it for others. Allâh says,

﴿أَفَلَا يَتَدَبَّرُونَ ٱلْقُرْءَانَ وَلَوْ كَانَ مِنْ عِندِ غَيْرِ ٱللَّهِ لَوَجَدُواْ فِيهِ ٱخْتِلَٰفًا كَثِيرًا﴾

"Do they not then consider the Qur'ân carefully? Had it been from other than Allâh, they would surely have found therein many contradictions."[2]

Five: The religion should include what can preserve for people, their religion, honour, properties, lives and offspring through its commandments, prohibitions, deterrents and morals that it ordains to protect these five general factors.

Six: It should serve as a mercy for mankind and save them from their own injustices and the injustices they commit against one another through usurping others' rights and the general amenities or through misleading the weak at the hands of the strong. Allâh says while explaining the mercy that the Torah which was given to Prophet Mûsâ entails,

﴿وَلَمَّا سَكَتَ عَن مُّوسَى ٱلْغَضَبُ أَخَذَ ٱلْأَلْوَاحَ وَفِي نُسْخَتِهَا هُدًى وَرَحْمَةٌ لِّلَّذِينَ هُمْ لِرَبِّهِمْ يَرْهَبُونَ﴾

---

[1] Az-Zukhruf 43:45
[2] An-Nisâ' 4:82

"And when the anger of Mûsâ was calmed down, he took up the Tablets; and in their inscription was guidance and mercy for those who fear their Lord."[1]

He also says informing us about the message of Prophet 'Isâ (Jesus),

﴿وَلِنَجْعَلَهُ ءَايَةً لِّلنَّاسِ وَرَحْمَةً مِّنَّا﴾

"And (We wish) to appoint him as a sign to mankind and a mercy from Us."[2]

He says about Prophet Sâlih,

﴿قَالَ يَـٰقَوْمِ أَرَءَيْتُمْ إِن كُنتُ عَلَىٰ بَيِّنَةٍ مِّن رَّبِّى وَءَاتَىٰنِى مِنْهُ رَحْمَةً فَمَن يَنصُرُنِى مِنَ ٱللَّهِ إِنْ عَصَيْتُهُ﴾

"He said, 'O my people: Tell me, if I am (acting) on a clear proof from my Lord, and there has come to me a mercy (Prophethood) from Him, who will save me from Allâh if I disobey Him?'"[3]

He says about the Qur'ân,

﴿وَنُنَزِّلُ مِنَ ٱلْقُرْءَانِ مَا هُوَ شِفَآءٌ وَرَحْمَةٌ لِّلْمُؤْمِنِينَ﴾

"And We send down of the Qur'ân that which is a healing and a mercy to those who believe."[4]

Seven: It should entail guidance to the Law of Allâh, and teach man the intention of Allâh by that Law. It should also be able to tell man his origin and his final destination. Allâh says about the Torah,

---

[1] Al-A'râf 7:154
[2] Maryam 19:21
[3] Hûd 11:63
[4] Al-Isrâ' 17:82

﴿إِنَّآ أَنزَلۡنَا ٱلتَّوۡرَىٰةَ فِيهَا هُدٗى وَنُورٞ﴾

"Verily, We did send down the Torah, therein was guidance and light."[1]

He says about the Injeel (the Book given to 'Isâ),

﴿وَءَاتَيۡنَٰهُ ٱلۡإِنجِيلَ فِيهِ هُدٗى وَنُورٞ﴾

"And We gave him the Injeel, in which was guidance and light."[2]

He says about the Qur'ân,

﴿هُوَ ٱلَّذِيٓ أَرۡسَلَ رَسُولَهُۥ بِٱلۡهُدَىٰ وَدِينِ ٱلۡحَقِّ﴾

"It is He Who has sent His Messenger (Muhammad ﷺ) with guidance and the religion of truth."[3]

The true religion is the one that includes guidance to the Law of Allâh, gives peace and tranquillity to the mind, protect it from all insinuations, answers all its questions and resolves every problem.

Eight: It should call to noble characters and deeds like truthfulness, honesty, modesty, chastity and generosity. It should also prohibit bad conducts like disobedience to parents, killing innocent souls, all kinds of immoralities, lies, injustice, aggression, stinginess and sins.

Nine: It should be able to provide happiness for those who believe in it. Allâh says,

---

[1] Al-Mâ'idah 5:44
[2] Al-Mâ'idah 5:46
[3] At-Tawbah 9:33

﴿طه ٠ مَآ أَنزَلْنَا عَلَيْكَ ٱلْقُرْءَانَ لِتَشْقَىٰ﴾

"Tâ-Hâ. We have not sent down the Qur'ân unto you (O Muhammad) to cause you distress."[1]

It should also be in harmony with upright nature.

﴿فِطْرَتَ ٱللَّهِ ٱلَّتِي فَطَرَ ٱلنَّاسَ عَلَيْهَا﴾

"(This is) Allâh's nature upon which He has created mankind."[2]

It must also be in harmony with sound reason, because the true religion is legislated by Allâh and the sound reason is created by Allâh and it is therefore impossible that the Law of Allâh and the creatures of Allâh should contradict each other.

Ten: It should lead to the truth, warn against falsehood, keep people away from error and lead them to the Straight Path where there is no crookedness. Allâh speaks about the *jinn* that when they heard the Qur'ân being recited, some of them told others,

﴿قَالُوا۟ يَٰقَوْمَنَآ إِنَّا سَمِعْنَا كِتَٰبًا أُنزِلَ مِنۢ بَعْدِ مُوسَىٰ مُصَدِّقًا لِّمَا بَيْنَ يَدَيْهِ يَهْدِىٓ إِلَى ٱلْحَقِّ وَإِلَىٰ طَرِيقٍ مُّسْتَقِيمٍ﴾

"O our people! Verily! We have heard a Book (the Qur'ân) sent down after Mûsâ, confirming what came before it: It guides to the truth and the Straight Path."[3]

It should not call to what will cause people misery, as Allâh says about the Qur'ân,

---

[1] Tâ-Hâ 20:1-2
[2] Ar-Rûm 30:30
[3] Al-Ahqâf 46:30

﴿طه ٠ مَآ أَنزَلْنَا عَلَيْكَ ٱلْقُرْءَانَ لِتَشْقَىٰٓ﴾

"Tâ-Hâ. We have not sent down the Qur'ân unto you to cause you distress."[1]

The true religion should also not enjoin on people what can cause them destruction. Allâh says,

﴿وَلَا تَقْتُلُوٓاْ أَنفُسَكُمْ إِنَّ ٱللَّهَ كَانَ بِكُمْ رَحِيمًا﴾

"And do not kill yourselves. Surely, Allâh is the Most-Merciful to you."[2]

It should also not distinguish between its adherents on the basis of race, colour or clan. Allâh says,

﴿يَٰٓأَيُّهَا ٱلنَّاسُ إِنَّا خَلَقْنَٰكُم مِّن ذَكَرٍ وَأُنثَىٰ وَجَعَلْنَٰكُمْ شُعُوبًا وَقَبَآئِلَ لِتَعَارَفُوٓاْ إِنَّ أَكْرَمَكُمْ عِندَ ٱللَّهِ أَتْقَىٰكُمْ إِنَّ ٱللَّهَ عَلِيمٌ خَبِيرٌ﴾

"O mankind! We have created you from a male and a female and made you into nations and tribes, that you may know one another. Verily, the most honourable of you with Allâh is that (believer) who is most pious. Verily, Allâh is All-Knowing, All-Aware."[3]

Therefore, the recognised criterion for giving people precedence in the true religion is piety.

After mentioning the criteria for distinguishing between the true religion and the false ones and citing evidences from the Qur'ân that these criteria are general in the case of all truthful Messengers sent by Allâh, it is then very appropriate to mention types of religion.

---

[1] Tâ-Hâ 20:1-2
[2] An-Nisâ' 4:29
[3] Al-Hujurât 49:13

Types of Religions

Mankind are divided as far as their faiths are concerned into two categories:

A category that have a Book that was revealed to them like the Jews, Christians and Muslims. As for the Jews and Christians, the Books that were revealed to their Prophets have been lost as a result of their ignorance of what was in their Books; their taking of men as gods beside Allâh and the long time that had passed between them and their acquaintance with these Books. So their priests wrote some books which they claimed to be from Allâh while they were not from Allâh but only wrong assumptions of liars and distortion of fanatics.

As for the Book of the Muslims (the Noble Qur'ân), it is the last Divine Book to be revealed and the strongest and most firm. Allâh Himself guaranteed its preservation and did not delegate that to mankind. He says,

$$ ﴿إِنَّا نَحْنُ نَزَّلْنَا ٱلذِّكْرَ وَإِنَّا لَهُ لَحَٰفِظُونَ﴾ $$

"Verily, We it is, Who has sent down the Dhikr (i.e., Qur'aan) and surely, We will guard it."[1]

The Qur'ân is therefore preserved in the hearts of people and in the Book, for it is the last Book which Allâh has guaranteed for the guidance of mankind. He has made it a proof against them till the Last Hour and has decreed its perpetuity. He provides for it in every

---

[1] Al-Hijr 15:9.

age those who will observe its limits and words, act by its law and believe in it. Further explanations about this Book will be given in a later section.

There is another section of religious adherents who have no revealed Book from Allâh, even though they possess an inherited book which is attributed to the founder of the religion like Hindus, Magians, Buddhists, Confucians and Arabs before the advent of Muhammad.

There is not a nation that does not have some knowledge and carry out some activities by which their worldly interests are achieved. This is the general knowledge which Allâh endowed every human being, even animals; for the animal is also guided as to how to attain what benefits it like food and drink and to avert what harms it; and Allâh has created in it the love for the former and aversion for the latter. He says,

$$﴿سَبِّحِ ٱسْمَ رَبِّكَ ٱلْأَعْلَى ٱلَّذِى خَلَقَ فَسَوَّىٰ وَٱلَّذِى قَدَّرَ فَهَدَىٰ﴾$$

"Glorify the Name of your Lord, the Most High, Who has created (everything) and then proportioned it. And Who has measured (preordainment for everything), and guided (i.e., showed mankind the right as well as the wrong paths and guided the animals to pasture)."[1]

He also says, informing us of what Prophet Mûsâ told Pharaoh,

$$﴿قَالَ رَبُّنَا ٱلَّذِىٓ أَعْطَىٰ كُلَّ شَىْءٍ خَلْقَهُ ثُمَّ هَدَىٰ﴾$$

---

[1] Al-A'lâ 87:1-3.

"Our Lord is He Who gave to each things its form and nature, then guided it aright."[1]

He also informs us about Prophet Ibrahîm that he said of His Lord,

$$﴿ ٱلَّذِى خَلَقَنِى فَهُوَ يَهْدِينِ ﴾$$

"Who has created me and it is He Who guides me."[2]

It is known to every sane person - who has the least reflection and sense of thinking - that adherents of religions are better in useful sciences and righteous deeds than those with no religion. There is therefore, no good thing found with non-Muslims among adherents of other religions except that the Muslims possess what is better and more perfect, so the adherents of religions possess what others do not possess. For sciences and deeds are two types:

First:
That which is achieved through intelligence and reason like astronomy, medical sciences and vocations. Though adherents of religions and atheists are equal in possession of these things; the adherents of religions are better in them. As for those things that cannot be known through mere reason like theology and religious sciences, these are prerogatives of the followers of religions. There are among this kind of knowledge that which can be proved by logical evidences, so the Messengers guided men unto how logical evidences proof that; which is both logical and legal.

---

[1] Tâ-Hâ 20:50.
[2] Ash-Shuaraa 26:78, See: *Al-Jawaab As-Saheeh* 4, Page 97.

Second:

What cannot be known except through the information given by the Messengers. This kind of knowledge and deeds cannot be achieved through human reason, like knowledge about Allâh, His Names and Attributes, the bliss that is in the Hereafter for whoever obeys Allâh and the punishment for those who disobey Him, the explanations on His injunctions and the information about the past Prophets and their peoples and so on.[1]

---

[1] See *Majmoo' Fataawaa Shaikhul Islâm* 4 p. 210-211.

Conditions of the Existing Religions

Great religions, their old books and ancient laws have become easy preys to frivolous and fraudulent people, an object of mockery for distorters and hypocrites and targets of bloody incidences and great calamities so much so that they have lost their spirit and shape. If their first adherents and prophets were to be resurrected now, they would surely have denied them and proclaimed to be ignorant of them.

Judaism[1] - today - has become a set of rituals and traditions with no spirit or life. Apart from this, it is a racial religion peculiar to a particular race and carries no message for the world, nor any mission for the people or any mercy for mankind.

This religion has been afflicted in its fundamental creed which is its motto among other religions and nations. And it has been a noble religion while it was the religion of monotheism which Prophets Ibrahîm and Ya'qûb commanded their children to follow. The Jews had adopted many concepts from the beliefs of corrupt nations with whom they shared neighbourhood or under whose authority they had been subjected. They had also adopted a lot of pagan customs and traditions of these people. This has been confirmed by unbiased Jewish historians. In Jewish

---

[1] For further reading, see the book, "Ifhaam al-Yahood" by Samuel bin Yahya Al-Maghrabi. He was a Jew who reverted to Islâm.

Encyclopaedia, we can read in it what approximately means,

"The Prophet's wrath over the worship of images does indicate that worshipping idols and false deities had crept into the hearts of the Israelites and that they had embraced the polytheistic and superstitious beliefs. The Talmud also testifies to the fact that paganism has a particular attraction for the Jews."[1]

The Babel Talmud[2] - which the Jews extremely hallow and prefer to the Torah, was widely circulated among the Jews of the Sixth Century, and which contains a lot of strange manifestations of their simple-mindedness, absurd sayings, insolent behaviour towards Allâh, scorning the reality and gambling with religion and human intellect - shows the extent to which the Jewish community of this age has degenerated intellectually and religiously.[3]

As for Christianity[4], it is also afflicted since its earliest days with distortions of extremists, alterations

---

[1] See Jewish Encyclopedia Vol. XLL. P 568-569

[2] The word 'Talmud' means, 'Jewish book of religious and moral teachings'. It is a compilation of footnotes and commentaries on their book 'Mishna' which means, 'the law' according to Jewish scholars of different generations.

[3] Read for information, "Al-Yahood alaa Hasab al-Talmud", by Dr. Rohlange and its translation from French to Arabic in "Al-kanzul marsood fee qawaaidit-talmood" by Yoosuf Hanna Nasrullaah.

[4] * For details, read, "Al-jawaab as-Saheeh liman baddala deenal-maseeh" by Shaykhul Islâm Ibn Taymiyyah; "Izhaar al-Haqq" by Rahmatullaah Al-Hindee and "Tuhfatul-Areeb fee radd 'alaa ubbaad As-Saleeb", by Abdullah At-Turjumaan who was a Christian revert.

of the ignorant and paganism of the Romans who claimed to be Christians.[1]

All these distortions, alterations and paganism have become the heap under which all great teachings of Christ were buried and the light of Monotheism and sincere worship of Allâh were hidden behind these clouds.

A Christian writer speaks on the extent to which the Trinity had gone in the Christian society since the end of the Fourth Century after Christ:

"The belief that one God consists of three different godheads had penetrated into the inner life of the Christian world and its thoughts since the last quarter of the fourth century and had become the official recognised creed in all parts of the Christendom ever since. Also, the development of Trinity and its secret were not revealed until in the last half of the nineteenth century A.D."[2]

A contemporary Christian historian[3] discusses in a book, *"History of Christianity in the Light of Modern Science"*, about the appearance of paganism in the Christian society in different forms and shapes and the Christians' diversity in adopting religious rites,

---

[1] See *"The Struggle between Religion and Science"*, (p.40-41) by the well-known European author Draper (Note: The translator does not know the actual name of this book in its original language nor the correct spelling of the name of its author because both were translated and transliterated respectively from Arabic).

[2] See *New Catholic Encyclopaedia, The Holy Trinity* Vol. 14 p. 295.

[3] Rev James Houston Baxter, *"History of Christianity in the Light of Modern Knowledge"*, Glasgow 1929 p. 407.

customs and pagan heroes of nations and religions
that are ancient in idolatry under the pretext of
imitation, admiration or ignorance. He said,
"Paganism has ended but has not been completely
eliminated. Rather, it has penetrated the hearts and
everything in it has been tolerantly allowed to
continue in the name of Christianity and under its
cover. Those who abandoned their gods and heroes
took one of their martyrs and gave him the title of their
former gods then erected a statue in his name. This is
how polytheism and idol worship are transferred unto
these local martyrs. By the end of that century,
worshipping of the martyrs and saints spread all
over the Christendom and formed a new creed that
teaches that saints have divine attributes. These saints
and hallowed men were thus made intermediaries
between God and man and pagan festivals were given
new names until the ancient pagan Sun festival was
turned to Christmas in the year 400 A.C."

As regards the Magians, they have been known
since time of old to be worshippers of natural
elements, the greatest of which is fire. They have
lately adhered to its worship and built for it alters
and temples so much so that fire houses have
become widespread in all places in their country and
all other religions and faiths disappear except fire
worship and hallowing of the sun. The religion,
according to these people has become mere rites and
traditions that are practised in special places.[1]

---

[1] Read the book, *"Iran During the Reign of Sasanids"* by
Professor of Eastern Languages at Copenhagen University,
Denmark, and a specialist on the history of Iran. See also,
"History of Iran" by the Magian, Shaeen Makareus.

The Danish author who wrote the book, "Iran During the Reign of Sasanids", describes their religious leaders and their functions, "These functionaries must worship fire four times in a day. In addition to this, they also worshipped moon, fire and water. They had an order that they should not let the fire die out or let the fire and water meet each other or let the metal rust, because they also hallow the metal."[1]

These Magians have practised dualism all the time and that has become their motto. They believed in two gods; god of light or god of good which they called "ahur mazda" or "Yazdan" and the other god is god of darkness or evil, and this they called: "ahur man". The war and conflict are continuously going between both of them.[2]

As regards Buddhism, the religion that is widespread in India and Middle Asia, it is a paganism whereof its adherents carry with them idols wherever they go. They build temples for these idols and erect the statue of "Buddha" wherever they go and settle.[3]

As for Hinduism the religion, of India, it has been popular with a lot of deities. Their paganism had reached its peak in the sixth century A.C. when the number of their deities reached 330 million gods.[4]

---

[1] *Iran During the Reign of Sasanids*, p. 155

[2] *Iran During the Reign of Sasanids*. p. 183-233.

[3] See *"The Ancient India"*, by Aishura Toba, a professor of Hindu Civilization at the University of Haydrabad; and *"The Discovery of India"* by Jawahar lal Nehru, the former Indian Prime Minister. p. 201-202.

[4] See *"Ancient India"* by R. Dit, 3/287; and *"The Prevailing Hinduism"*, by L.S.S.O. Malley p. 6-7.

Everything according to Brahmanism has become wonderful and everything has become useful and a deity to be worshipped. During that age, the art of idol making became highly profitable and many idol stylists carved so many idols in different shapes.

The Hindi writer, C. V. Vidya, wrote in his book, *"The History of Medieval Hindu"* while discussing the era of King Harsh (606-648 A.D.), which is the era that follows the advent of Islâm in Arabia,

"Hinduism and Buddhism are equally pagan religion though Buddhism might have surpassed Hinduism in paganism. The origin of Buddhism was denial of existence of any Lord but it gradually adopted Buddha (its founder) as the greatest deity. It later on added other deities like Bodhistavas. Paganism has reached its peak in India so much so that the name Buddha became synonymous with idol or statue in some eastern languages." It is without doubt that Paganism has become widespread in the conemporary world. The whole world from the Atlantic Sea to the Pacific Ocean is greatly immersed in Paganism. The matter becomes as if the Christianity, the Semitic religions and Buddhism are competing in glorification and hallowing of idols like racing horses.[1]

Another Hindu said in his book, *"The Prevailing Hinduism"*, that the art of making idols had not ended yet, but small idols continued to join the existing 'deities complex' in great numbers throughout different historical periods that they have

---

[1] C.V. Vidya: *History of Medieval Hindu*. Vol. I (Poone 1921)

become an innumerable and an uncountable thong of deities.[1]

This is the condition of the world religions. As for civilized countries where great governments were established, where many sciences flourished and which were the bedrock of civilization, industry and arts, they have become countries with no religions; countries that had lost their origin and power, in which there are no righteous reformers and teachers, where atheism is publicly proclaimed, corruption of all kind proliferated, all standards have been changed and the man has become valueless to his own self. That is why there are many cases of suicide, that all family links have been cut, social relations were put in disarray, the clinics of psychologists are jammed with patients and the market of magic tricksters were established. In these so-called civilized nations, man tries out of every enjoyable thing and follows every invented and innovated creed, seeking to satiate the demand of his soul, make himself happy and give himself peace of mind. But all these enjoyments, and all these creeds and theories failed to achieve these goals for him, and he shall continue in this psychological misery and spiritual torment until he establishes relationship with his Creator and worships Him according to the way He is pleased with and with which He sent His Messengers. Allâh says, while describing the condition of the one who turns away from his Lord and seeks for guidance from others besides Him,

---

[1] See "As-Seeratun-Nabawiyyah" by Abul Hasan An-Nadwi p. 19-28.

﴿وَمَنْ أَعْرَضَ عَن ذِكْرِى فَإِنَّ لَهُ مَعِيشَةً ضَنكًا وَنَحْشُرُهُ يَوْمَ ٱلْقِيَـٰمَةِ أَعْمَىٰ﴾

"But whosoever turns away from My Reminder (i.e., neither believes in this Qur'ân nor acts on its teachings) verily, for him is a life of hardship and We shall raise him up blind on the Day of Resurrection."[1]

He, may He be glorified, also informs us about the life of the true believers and their happiness in this worldly life when He says,

ٱلَّذِينَ ءَامَنُوا۟ وَلَمْ يَلْبِسُوٓا۟ إِيمَـٰنَهُم بِظُلْمٍ أُو۟لَـٰٓئِكَ لَهُمُ ٱلْأَمْنُ وَهُم مُّهْتَدُونَ﴾

"It is they who believe (in the Oneness of Allâh and worship none but Him alone) and confuse not their belief with wrong (by worshipping others besides Allâh), for them (only) there is security and they are the guided."[2]

He Whose praise is great also says,

﴿وَأَمَّا ٱلَّذِينَ سُعِدُوا۟ فَفِى ٱلْجَنَّةِ خَـٰلِدِينَ فِيهَا مَا دَامَتِ ٱلسَّمَـٰوَٰتُ وَٱلْأَرْضُ إِلَّا مَا شَآءَ رَبُّكَ عَطَآءً غَيْرَ مَجْذُوذٍ ﴾

"As for those who are blessed, they will be in Paradise, abiding therein for all the time that the heavens and the earth endure, except as your Lord wills; a gift without an end."[3]

---

[1] Tâ-Hâ 20:124.
[2] Al-An'âm 6:82
[3] Hûd 11:108.

If we apply the criteria of the true religion to all these religions - except Islâm, we will see that they are short of all these criteria as it is clear from the above exposition.

The greatest element which all these religions are short of is monotheism. For their adherents have associated other gods with Allâh in worship in addition to the fact that these religions do not provide people with a law that can be applicable in all places and at all times and that can protect them, their lives, faith, honour, offspring and properties. These religions also do not guide people to the Law of Allâh which He orders to be followed neither do they give their adherents peace of mind and happiness, as a result of their inherent contradictions.

As regards Islâm, you will come to know in the following chapters that it is the true religion of Allâh which He is pleased with and which He has chosen for mankind as their religion.

At the end of this section, it is appropriate that we define the essence of prophethood and the need of mankind for it; and explain the foundations of the mission of the Messengers and the reality of the last and everlasting message of Islâm.

The Essence of Prophethood

The greatest thing that man must know in this life is the knowledge about his Lord, Who created him from nothing and showered him with blessings. And the greatest purpose for which Allâh created the creation is to worship Him alone.

But how can man know his Lord as it is due? What are the duties and obligations binding on him? How can he worship his Lord? Man can find who will assist him during vicissitudes of life, provide for his needs like treatment for an ailment, giving some medicine, assisting to build a house and so on and so forth; but he cannot find among ordinary people who can make him know his Lord and explain to him how to worship Him. This is because human intelligence cannot independently know what Allâh intends, he cannot even perceive the intention of his fellow human being before he tells him what he intends. How can he then know what Allâh means? Further, it is also because, this matter is only restricted to the Messengers and Prophets whom Allâh has chosen to convey the Message and to those who come after them among the rightly guided leaders and the heirs of the Prophet, who follow their way, take to their Path and help to convey their message. For men cannot receive revelation from Allâh directly as they are unable to bear it. Allâh says,

﴿وَمَا كَانَ لِبَشَرٍ أَن يُكَلِّمَهُ اللَّهُ إِلَّا وَحْيًا أَوْ مِن وَرَآيِ حِجَابٍ أَوْ يُرْسِلَ رَسُولًا فَيُوحِيَ بِإِذْنِهِ مَا يَشَاءُ إِنَّهُ عَلِيٌّ حَكِيمٌ﴾

"It is not given to any human being that Allâh should speak to him unless (it be) by Revelation, or from behind a veil, or that He sends a Messenger to reveal what He wills by His leave. Verily, He is Most-High, Most Wise."[1]

There should therefore be an intermediary and an envoy who can convey the law of Allâh to His slaves, Those intermediaries and envoys are the Messengers and Prophets. The angel will carry the message to the Prophet and the Prophet will convey it to the people. The angels do not carry the message to men directly, for the world of angels is naturally different from that of human beings. Allâh says,

﴿ٱللَّهُ يَصۡطَفِى مِنَ ٱلۡمَلَٰٓئِكَةِ رُسُلًا وَمِنَ ٱلنَّاسِۚ﴾

"Allâh chooses Messengers from angels and from men."[2]

The Wisdom of Allâh necessitates that the Messenger should come from the race of those whom he is sent to, so that they could understand him because of their ability to speak with him. If Messengers had been sent to mankind from among the angels, they could not have been able to face him or learn anything from him. Allâh the exalted says,

﴿وَقَالُواْ لَوۡلَآ أُنزِلَ عَلَيۡهِ مَلَكٌۖ وَلَوۡ أَنزَلۡنَا مَلَكًا لَّقُضِىَ ٱلۡأَمۡرُ ثُمَّ لَا يُنظَرُونَ ○ وَلَوۡ جَعَلۡنَٰهُ مَلَكًا لَّجَعَلۡنَٰهُ رَجُلًا وَلَلَبَسۡنَا عَلَيۡهِم مَّا يَلۡبِسُونَ﴾

---

[1] Ash-Shûrâ 42:51.

[2] Al-Hajj 22:75.

"And they say: Why has not an angel been sent down to him? Had we sent down an angel, the matter would have been judged at once, and no respite would be granted to them. And had We appointed him an angel, We indeed would have made him a man, and We would have certainly confused them in which they are already confused."[1]

He also says,

وَمَآ أَرْسَلْنَا قَبْلَكَ مِنَ ٱلْمُرْسَلِينَ إِلَّآ إِنَّهُمْ لَيَأْكُلُونَ ٱلطَّعَامَ وَيَمْشُونَ فِي ٱلْأَسْوَاقِ وَجَعَلْنَا بَعْضَكُمْ لِبَعْضٍ فِتْنَةً أَتَصْبِرُونَ وَكَانَ رَبُّكَ بَصِيرًا ۝ وَقَالَ ٱلَّذِينَ لَا يَرْجُونَ لِقَآءَنَا لَوْلَآ أُنزِلَ عَلَيْنَا ٱلْمَلَٰٓئِكَةُ أَوْ نَرَىٰ رَبَّنَا لَقَدِ ٱسْتَكْبَرُوا۟ فِي أَنفُسِهِمْ وَعَتَوْ عُتُوًّا كَبِيرًا

"And We never sent before you (O Muhammad ﷺ) any of the Messengers but verily, they ate food and walked in the markets. And We have made some of you as a trial for others: will you have patience? And your Lord is Ever All-Seer (of everything). And those who expect not a meeting with Us (i.e., those who deny the Day of Resurrection and the life of the Hereafter) said: 'Why are not the angels sent down to us, or why do we not see our Lord?' Indeed, they think too highly of themselves and are scornful with great pride."[2]

He also says,

وَمَآ أَرْسَلْنَا مِن قَبْلِكَ إِلَّا رِجَالًا نُّوحِيٓ إِلَيْهِمْ فَسْـَٔلُوٓا۟ أَهْلَ ٱلذِّكْرِ إِن كُنتُمْ لَا تَعْلَمُونَ

---

[1] Al-An'âm 6:8-9.
[2] Al-Furqân 25:20-21.

"And We sent not (as Our Messengers) before you (O Muhammad ﷺ) any but men."[1]

He also says,

$$﴿وَمَآ أَرْسَلْنَا مِن رَّسُولٍ إِلَّا بِلِسَانِ قَوْمِهِۦ لِيُبَيِّنَ لَهُمْ فَيُضِلُّ اللَّهُ مَن يَشَآءُ وَيَهْدِى مَن يَشَآءُ وَهُوَ الْعَزِيزُ الْحَكِيمُ﴾$$

"And We sent not a Messenger except with the language of his people, in order that he might make the Message clear to them."[2]

These Messengers and Prophets possessed complete and perfect reason, sound nature, truthfulness in words and deeds, sincerity in conveying what was put in their trust, Divine immunity from all that could tarnish human conduct and physical appearances that are free from all things that are repugnant to sights and repulsive to sound human taste.[3] Allâh purified them in their persons and manners. They are the most perfect in manners, purest in souls and most generous. Allâh combined in them good manners and excellent conduct as He combined in them deliberateness, knowledge, magnanimity, generosity, bravery and justice. By these qualities, they were distinguished among their peoples. The people of Prophet Sâlih told him as Allâh informs us in His Book,

$$﴿قَالُوا يَـٰصَـٰلِحُ قَدْ كُنتَ فِينَا مَرْجُوًّا قَبْلَ هَـٰذَآ أَتَنْهَـٰنَآ أَن نَّعْبُدَ مَا يَعْبُدُ ءَابَآؤُنَا﴾$$

---

[1] An-Nahl 16:43.

[2] Ibrâhîm 14:4.

[3] See: *Lawaami'ul anwaar al bahiyyah* Vol. 2 pp. 265 and, "Al-Islâm" by Ahmad Shalabee p. 114.

"They said: 'O Sâlih! You have been among us as a figure of good hope till this (new thing which you have brought that we leave our gods and worship your God [Allâh] alone). Do you now forbid us the worship of what our fathers have worshipped?' "[1]

He also informs us of what the people of Prophet Shu'aib told him,

$$﴿قَالُوا يَٰشُعَيْبُ أَصَلَوٰتُكَ تَأْمُرُكَ أَن نَّتْرُكَ مَا يَعْبُدُ ءَابَاؤُنَا أَوْ أَن نَّفْعَلَ فِي أَمْوَٰلِنَا مَا نَشَٰؤُا إِنَّكَ لَأَنتَ ٱلْحَلِيمُ ٱلرَّشِيدُ﴾$$

"They said: 'O Shu'aib! Does your prayers command that we give up what our fathers used to worship, or that we give up doing what we like with our property. Verily, you are the forbearer, right-minded.' "[2]

The Messenger of Allâh, Muhammad, was also popular among his people with the title *"Al-Ameen"* (the trustworthy) even before he received the revelation, His Lord describes him saying,

$$﴿وَإِنَّكَ لَعَلَىٰ خُلُقٍ عَظِيمٍ﴾$$

"And verily, you (O Muhammad) are on an exalted (standard) of character."[3]

The Messengers and Prophets are therefore, the best ones among Allâh's creatures. He selected them and chose them to carry His Message and convey it to mankind, and,

$$﴿ٱللَّهُ أَعْلَمُ حَيْثُ يَجْعَلُ رِسَالَتَهُۥ﴾$$

---

[1] Hûd 11:62.
[2] Hûd 11:87.
[3] Al-Qalam 68:4.

"Allâh knows best with whom to place His Message."[1]

Allâh says,

﴿إِنَّ ٱللَّهَ ٱصْطَفَىٰٓ ءَادَمَ وَنُوحًا وَءَالَ إِبْرَٰهِيمَ وَءَالَ عِمْرَٰنَ عَلَى ٱلْعَٰلَمِينَ﴾

"Allâh chose Adam, Noah, the family of Ibrâhîm and the family of Imrân above the mankind (of their time)."[2]

These Messengers and Prophets - in spite of lofty qualities with which Allâh described them and the excellent conducts for which they were known - are nevertheless humans who suffered what other humans suffer; they suffered hunger and sickness; they slept, ate, married and died. Allâh says, addressing Prophet Muhammad ﷺ,

﴿إِنَّكَ مَيِّتٌ وَإِنَّهُم مَّيِّتُونَ﴾

"Verily, you will die, and verily, they (too) will die."[3]

Allâh also says,

﴿وَلَقَدْ أَرْسَلْنَا رُسُلًا مِّن قَبْلِكَ وَجَعَلْنَا لَهُمْ أَزْوَٰجًا وَذُرِّيَّةً﴾

"And indeed, We sent Messengers before you (O Muhammad) and made for them wives and offspring."[4]

They were even subjected to persecution; many of

---

[1] Al-An'âm 6:124.
[2] Aal Imrân 3:33.
[3] Az-Zumar 39:30.
[4] Ar-Ra'd 13:38.

them were killed or expelled from their homes. Allâh says addressing Prophet Muhammad ﷺ,

$$﴿وَإِذْ يَمْكُرُ بِكَ ٱلَّذِينَ كَفَرُوا لِيُثْبِتُوكَ أَوْ يَقْتُلُوكَ أَوْ يُخْرِجُوكَ وَيَمْكُرُونَ وَيَمْكُرُ ٱللَّهُ وَٱللَّهُ خَيْرُ ٱلْمَٰكِرِينَ﴾$$

"And remember when the disbelievers plotted against you to imprison you, or to kill you or to expel you (from your home), they were plotting and Allâh too was plotting; and Allâh is the Best of those who plot."[1]

But to them were the end, victory and authority in this worldly life and the Hereafter. Allâh says,

$$﴿وَلَيَنصُرَنَّ ٱللَّهُ مَن يَنصُرُهُۥ﴾$$

"Allâh will help those who help His (cause)."[2]

He also says,

$$﴿كَتَبَ ٱللَّهُ لَأَغْلِبَنَّ أَنَا۠ وَرُسُلِي إِنَّ ٱللَّهَ قَوِيٌّ عَزِيزٌ﴾$$

"Allâh has decreed: Verily, it is I and My Messengers who shall be the victorious. Verily, Allâh is All-Powerful, All-Mighty."[3]

---

[1] Al-Anfâl 8:30.
[2] Al-Hajj 22:40.
[3] Al-Mujâdilah 58:21.

Signs of Prophethood

Since Prophethood is a means by which the noblest of all knowledge can be acquired and the greatest and most honourable deeds can be carried out; it is of Allâh's mercy to give these Prophets the signs by which they could be known and through which they could be identified, though, every one of those who claimed to have a mission has some signs and conditions that could indicate his truthfulness if he is truthful or otherwise if he is a liar. Theses signs are many, the most important of which are:

1. The Messenger should call to the worship of Allâh alone and to the abandonment of worshipping others besides Him. For this is the purpose for which Allâh created the creation.

2. The Messenger should call people to believe in him, and put his message into practice. Allâh commands His Messenger, Muhammad ﷺ to say,

﴿قُلْ يَٰٓأَيُّهَا ٱلنَّاسُ إِنِّى رَسُولُ ٱللَّهِ إِلَيْكُمْ جَمِيعًا﴾

"O mankind! Verily, I am sent to you all as the Messenger of Allâh."[1]

3. Allâh strengthens him with various kinds of signs of prophethood. Among these signs are the Verses that the Prophet Muhammad brought from Allâh and which his people could not repudiate or produce its like. Another example is the sign of Prophet Mûsâ when his rod turned to a snake; the sign of Prophet

---

[1] Al-A'râf 7:158.

Îsâ who healed the blind and the leper by the permission of Allâh, and the sign of Muhammad which is the Great Qur'ân, in spite of the fact that he was an illiterate who could neither read nor write among many other signs of the Prophets.

Among these signs is the clear and vivid truth which the Prophets and Messengers (peace be upon them) brought and which their opponents could not disprove or deny. Rather, their opponents knew that what the Prophets had brought was the truth that could not be resisted.

Among the signs also are perfect conditions, beautiful traits and magnanimous conduct with which Allâh distinguished the Prophets.

4. His message should agree in fundamentals with the fundamentals to which all Messengers and Prophets called.[1]

5. He should not call others to the worship of himself or to direct any act of worship to him. He should also not call to the glorification of his tribe or clan. Allâh commands His Prophet Muhammad ﷺ to tell people,

﴿قُل لَّا أَقُولُ لَكُمْ عِندِى خَزَآئِنُ ٱللَّهِ وَلَآ أَعْلَمُ ٱلْغَيْبَ وَلَآ أَقُولُ لَكُمْ إِنِّي مَلَكٌ إِنْ أَتَّبِعُ إِلَّا مَا يُوحَىٰ إِلَيَّ﴾

"Say: I do not tell you that with me is the treasure of Allâh, nor (that) I know the Unseen; nor I tell you that I am an angel. I but follow what is revealed to me."[2]

---

[1] See: Majmoo' Fataawa Ibn Taymiyyah Vol. 4 p. 212-213.
[2] Al-An'âm 6:50.

6. He should not ask from people any of the things of this world as a wage for his mission. Allâh says, informing us about His Prophets Noah, Hûd, Sâlih, Lût and Shu'aib, that they told their people,

﴿وَمَا أَسْأَلُكُمْ عَلَيْهِ مِنْ أَجْرٍ إِنْ أَجْرِيَ إِلَّا عَلَىٰ رَبِّ ٱلْعَٰلَمِينَ﴾

"No reward do I ask of you for it (my message of Islâmic Monotheism); my reward is only from the Lord of all that exists."[1]

Prophet Muhammad also told his people,

﴿قُلْ مَا أَسْأَلُكُمْ عَلَيْهِ مِنْ أَجْرٍ وَمَا أَنَا مِنَ ٱلْمُتَكَلِّفِينَ﴾

"No wage do I ask of you this (the Qur'ân) nor am I of those who pretend and fabricate things.."[2]

These Prophets and Messengers whom I have told you something of their qualities and signs of their prophethood, are many. Allâh says,

﴿وَلَقَدْ بَعَثْنَا فِى كُلِّ أُمَّةٍ رَّسُولًا أَنِ ٱعْبُدُوا۟ ٱللَّهَ وَٱجْتَنِبُوا۟ ٱلطَّٰغُوتَ﴾

"And verily, We have sent among every nation a Messenger (proclaiming): Worship Allâh (Alone) and avoid all false deities."[3]

These Messengers have made mankind happy; the history recorded their stories and the injunctions of their religion were repeatedly transmitted, that they are the truth and just. Likewise, repeatedly narrated is

---

[1] Ash-Shu'araa 26:109, 127, 145, 164, 180.
[2] Saad 38:86.
[3] An-Nahl 16:36.

the victory with which Allâh honoured them and destruction of their enemies, like the destruction of the people of Noah with flood, drowning of Pharaoh, punishment for the people of Lût; and the victory of Muhammad over his enemies and the spread of his religion. Whoever knows this will know certainly that they brought for mankind good and guidance; that they directed them to all that could benefit them and warn them against all that could be harmful. The first of them is Adam and the last is Muhammad.

Mankind's Need for the Messengers

The Prophets are Allâh's Messengers to His slaves; they convey His commandments to them, they give them glad tidings of the bliss which Allâh has prepared for them if they obey His Commandments, warn them of the everlasting punishment if they disobey Him and tell them the stories of the past nations and what befell them of the punishment and torment in this world because they disobeyed the commandments of their Lord.

These Divine Commandments and prohibitions cannot be known independently by human reasoning, that is why Allâh ordained and prescribed commandments and prohibitions as a honour for mankind and to protect his interests. For people tend to obey their desires, thereby violating forbidden things, attacking other people and usurping their rights. It is therefore out of the utmost wisdom too that Allâh should send Messengers among mankind, every now and then, who would remind them of the commandments of Allâh, warn them against disobedience, recite to them admonitions and tell them the stories of past generations. Because, when wonderful stories are heard and marvellous concepts awaken the psyche, the sense of reason embraces that, increases in knowledge and has right perception. The more man listens the more he thinks; the more he thinks the more he reflects; the more he reflects the more he understands and the more he understands the more he acts. So, sending Messengers is inevitable and there is no alternative for them if the truth is to be established.[1]

Shaykhul Islâm Ibn Taymiyyah[2] said, "Divine Message is necessary for reformation of man in his worldly life and his final abode. As there will not be well-being for him in his Hereafter if he does not follow the message, there will also not be well-being for him in his worldly life if he does not follow the Message. He is therefore, bound to follow the Law of Allâh for he lives between two movements: a movement by which he seeks what benefits him and another by which he wards off what harms him. The Law of Allâh is then the light that shows him what can benefit or harm him. That is the Light of Allâh on the earth, His justice between His slaves and His fortress which provides safety for whoever enters it. What is meant by the Law of Allâh is not physical distinction between the harmful and useful; for even the animals can do that. The donkey or camel can differentiate between barley and sand. What is meant by that is to be able to distinguish between deeds that can harm their doer in his worldly life and his Hereafter and deeds that can benefit him in his worldly life and his Hereafter. Like the benefit of faith, belief in the Oneness of Allâh, justice, righteousness, kindness, honesty, chastity, courage, knowledge, perseverance,

---

[1] A'laam An-Nubuwwa by 'Alee bin Muhammad Al-Mawardee p. 33.

[2] He is Ahmad bin Abdul-Haleem, popularly known as Ibn Taymiyyah. He was born in the year 661 A.H. and died in the year 728 A.H. He was one of the great Islâmic Scholars and the author of many valuable books.

enjoining all that is good, forbidding all that is evil, being kind to the kith and kin, being dutiful to parents, being kind to neighbours, fulfilling obligations, purifying deeds for Allâh, putting trust in Him, seeking help from Him, being pleased with His pre-decrees, submission to His rule, believing in Him and His Messengers in all that they inform him and all other deeds that are beneficial to man in his worldly life and his Hereafter. In the opposite of the above lies his misery and harm in his worldly life and his Hereafter.

Had it not been because of the Divine Message, the human intellect would have not been guided to the details of what could benefit or harm him in his worldly life. Among the greatest favours of Allâh upon His slaves is that He sent His Messengers to them, revealed to them His Books and showed them the Straight Path. Had it not been for this, humans would have been like cattle or even worse. So, whoever accepts the message of Allâh and stands firm on that is among the best of all creation. But whoever rejects it and deviates from it, such is among the worst of the creation and worse in condition than the dog and pig and the most contemptible creature. There is no way the inhabitants of the earth can survive except by the effects of the message that is existent among them, for when the impacts of the message become exterminated from the earth and the signs of their guidance become wiped off, Allâh will dismantle the heaven and the earth and bring forth the Resurrection.

Further, the dweller of the earth need for the Message

is not like their need for sun, moon, air and rain, and it
is also not like their need for their own souls or like the
need of the eye for the light; or like that of the body for
food and drink. Rather the need for the Messenger is
greater than all that and all other things one could
think of or assume. The Messengers are the
intermediary between Allâh and His creatures as far
as His commandment and prohibitions are concerned;
they are the envoys between Him and His slaves. The
last of them, their leader and the dearest of them to
Allâh is Muhammad ﷺ. Allâh sent him as mercy for
mankind and all that exists. He makes him a proof for
the followers of the Right Path and a proof against all
creatures. He commanded His slaves to follow, love,
respect and honour him, and to give him all
obligations due to him. Allâh took covenants and
pledges from all other Prophets and Messengers that
they would believe in and follow him (if they were to
meet him or hear of him) and He also ordered them to
take the same covenant from their believing followers.
Allâh sent him at the threshold of the Hour. With him,
He guided many from error, rescued many from
ignorance, and opened through his Message blind
eyes, deaf ears and sealed hearts. He lightened the
earth through his message, after it had been in
darkness and united with it the separated hearts. He
straightened with the Messenger the crooked faith and
explained through him the bright path. Allâh opened
for him his heart, removed from him his burden,
raised high his fame and subjected those who were
against him to humiliation and disgrace. He sent him
after a break in the succession of the sent Messengers
and extermination of the impacts of the previously

revealed Books; when words had been twisted and the law altered, when every nation relied on injustice in their opinions, made decisions regarding Allâh and between His slaves with their own corrupt sayings and desires. It was then that Allâh guided mankind through him and showed them the right way, He brought people from darkness to light through him and made distinction with him, between those who deserve success and those who were sinners. Whoever follows his guidance will be rightly guided and whoever deviates from His Path will go astray and such has only oppressed himself. May Allâh bestow peace and blessings on him and all other Messengers and Prophets.[1]

We can now summarise man's need for the message in the following points:

1. That man is a nurtured creature and it is inevitable for him to know his Lord and Creator; to know what He wants from him and why He created him. Man cannot however know all that independently except by knowing the Prophets and the Messengers and knowing the guidance and light which they brought.

2. Man is a component of body and soul. The nutrition for body is whatever is available of food and drink, but the nutrition of the soul has been prescribed by the One Who created it; that nutrition is true religion and righteous deed. So it is the Prophets and Messengers who brought true reli-

---

[1] Qaa'idah fee wujoobil I'tisaam bir-risaalah by Ibn Taymiyyah, See: Al-Fataawaa 19 p.99-102.

gion and guided to righteous deed.

3. Man is religious by nature and he must have a religion which he must practice and this religion must be the true one. So, there is no way to know the true religion except through belief in the Prophets and Messengers and to believe in all that they brought.

4. Man is in need of knowing the way that can lead him to the pleasure of Allâh in this world and to His Paradise and bliss in the Hereafter. And no one can guide to this way except the Prophets and Messengers alone.

5. Man is in himself weak and many enemies lay in wait for him: Satan wants to mislead him, evil companions make bad things fair-seeming to him and his base self incites him to do evil. Hence, he needs what can protect him against the evil plans of his enemies and it is the Prophets and Messengers who guided man to that and clearly explained it to him.

6. Man is civil by nature, his meeting with people and his relations with them therefore need a law by which justice and equality can be established among people - the absence of which can make human life be like that of the jungle. Also, this law must be able to protect the right of every one without excessiveness and negligence and none could bring such perfect law except the Messengers and Prophets.

7. Man needs to know what can give him tranquillity

and psychological security and guide him to means of real happiness. This is what the Prophets and Messengers guided to. After explaining why the creation is in need of Prophets and Messengers, it is now appropriate to discuss the final return and explain the proofs and evidences that support that.

The Final Return

Every man knows with certainty that death is inevitable. But what is his fate after death? Will he be happy or miserable?

Many people and nations of the world believe that they will be resurrected after death and called to account for all their deeds; that they will earn good reward if they do good and punishment if they do evil.[1] This issue - the Resurrection and accountability - are confirmed by sound reason and supported by Divine Laws. It is based on three fundamentals:

1. Confirmation of the perfect knowledge of the Lord, may He be glorified.

2. Confirmation of His perfect Omnipotence.

3. Confirmation of His perfect Wisdom.[2]

There are many textual and logical evidences on the confirmation of the final return some of which are:

1. Drawing evidence on the resurrection of the dead through the creation of the heavens and the earth. Allâh says,

﴿أَوَلَمْ يَرَوْا أَنَّ اللَّهَ الَّذِى خَلَقَ السَّمَٰوَٰتِ وَالْأَرْضَ وَلَمْ يَعْىَ بِخَلْقِهِنَّ بِقَٰدِرٍ عَلَىٰ أَن يُحْىِۦَ الْمَوْتَىٰ بَلَىٰٓ إِنَّهُۥ عَلَىٰ كُلِّ شَىْءٍ قَدِيرٌ﴾

"Do they not see that Allâh, Who created the heavens and the earth, and was not wearied by their creation,

---

[1] See: *Al-Jawaabus-Saheeh* Vol. 4 p. 96.
[2] See: *Al-Fawaaid* by Ibn al-Qayyim p. 6-7.

is Able to give life to the dead? Yes, He is surely Able to do all things."[1]

He also says,

﴿أَوَلَيْسَ ٱلَّذِى خَلَقَ ٱلسَّمَٰوَٰتِ وَٱلْأَرْضَ بِقَٰدِرٍ عَلَىٰٓ أَن يَخْلُقَ مِثْلَهُم بَلَىٰ وَهُوَ ٱلْخَلَّٰقُ ٱلْعَلِيمُ﴾

"Is not He Who created the heavens and the earth, is Able to create the like of them? Yes, indeed. He is the All-Knowing Supreme Creator."[2]

2. Drawing evidence of Allâh's ability to reproduce the creation once more from His ability to originate the creation without any previous example. So, He, Who is able to bring a thing into existence should be able to reproduce it with greater reason. Allâh the Exalted says,

﴿وَهُوَ ٱلَّذِى يَبْدَؤُا۟ ٱلْخَلْقَ ثُمَّ يُعِيدُهُۥ وَهُوَ أَهْوَنُ عَلَيْهِ وَلَهُ ٱلْمَثَلُ ٱلْأَعْلَىٰ﴾

"And He it is Who originates the creation, then He will repeat it (after it has been perished); and this is easier for Him. His is the Sublime Similitude."[3]

He also says,

﴿وَضَرَبَ لَنَا مَثَلًا وَنَسِىَ خَلْقَهُۥ قَالَ مَن يُحْىِ ٱلْعِظَٰمَ وَهِىَ رَمِيمٌ قُلْ يُحْيِيهَا ٱلَّذِىٓ أَنشَأَهَآ أَوَّلَ مَرَّةٍ وَهُوَ بِكُلِّ خَلْقٍ عَلِيمٌ﴾

"And he (man) puts forth for Us a parable, and has

[1] Al-Ahqâf 46:33.
[2] Yâ-Sîn 36:81.
[3] Ar-Rûm 30:27.

forgotten the facts of his own creation. He says: Who will give life to these bones after they are rotten and have become dust. Say (O Muhammad): He will give life to them Who created them at the first! And He is the All-Knower of every creation."[1]

3. He created man in the best shape and in this perfect and complete form. He endowed him with limbs, power and characteristics; with flesh, bones, veins and nerves; with outlets, tools, sciences, wishes and industries. There is in all this the greatest evidence of His ability to resurrect the dead.

4. Drawing the proof of His ability to resurrect the dead in the Hereafter, from His raising up of the dead in this worldly life. Stories have been narrated of this in the Divine Books which Allâh revealed to His Messengers. Examples of this is raising up the dead by the permission of Allâh at the hands of Prophets Ibrâhîm and 'Îsâ, may peace be upon them - among many others.

5. Drawing evidence of His ability to resurrect the dead from His ability to bring about things that are similar to the scenes of the Day of Congregation and Resurrection like:

a. Allâh created man from a drop of sperm that was scattered all over the body - that is why all parts of the body enjoy the intercourse - Allâh collects this drop from all parts of the body, then makes it go to the womb and created therewith the man. If all these parts were scattered and He gathered them

---

[1] Yâ-Sîn 36:78-79.

together and created from them that man, then if
they become scattered once again after death, what
can prevent Him from bringing them together once
more. Allâh says,

﴿أَفَرَءَيْتُم مَّا تُمْنُونَ ٠ءَأَنتُمْ تَخْلُقُونَهُۥٓ أَمْ نَحْنُ ٱلْخَٰلِقُونَ﴾

*"Then tell Me about the semen that you emit. Is it you
who create it (i.e., make this semen into a perfect
human being)? Or are We the Creator?"*[1]

b. When the plant seeds - regardless of their shapes -
   fall into the fertile land and water and soil
   overwhelm them; the logical consequence is that
   they become rotten and decayed; for, any of the
   water and soil is enough to make the seed rotten
   and the combination of both will can it so with
   greater reason. But the fact is that, the seed will not
   decay but remains preserved. When the humidity
   increases, the seed breaks open and from it comes
   out a plant. Does that not point to a perfect power
   and comprehensive wisdom? Will this All-Wise
   and All-Able Lord be incapable of collecting parts
   of man and reconstituting his limbs? Allâh says,

﴿أَفَرَءَيْتُم مَّا تَحْرُثُونَ ٠ءَأَنتُمْ تَزْرَعُونَهُۥٓ أَمْ نَحْنُ ٱلزَّٰرِعُونَ﴾

*"Then tell Me about the seed that you sow in the
ground. Is it you that make it grow, or are We the
Grower?"*[2]

A similar Verse in meaning is Allâh's saying,

---

[1] Al-Wâqi'ah 56:58-59.

[2] Al-Wâqi'ah 56:63-64.

﴿وَتَرَى ٱلْأَرْضَ هَامِدَةً فَإِذَآ أَنزَلْنَا عَلَيْهَا ٱلْمَآءَ ٱهْتَزَّتْ وَرَبَتْ وَأَنۢبَتَتْ مِن كُلِّ زَوْجٍ بَهِيجٍ﴾

"And you see the earth barren, but when We sent down water (rain) on it, it is stirred (to life) and it swells and puts forth every lovely kind (of growth)."[1]

6. The All-Able, All-Knowledgeable and All-Wise Creator is deemed far from producing the creation for fun and leaving them in vain. He says,

﴿وَمَا خَلَقْنَا ٱلسَّمَآءَ وَٱلْأَرْضَ وَمَا بَيْنَهُمَا بَٰطِلًا ذَٰلِكَ ظَنُّ ٱلَّذِينَ كَفَرُوا۟ فَوَيْلٌ لِّلَّذِينَ كَفَرُوا۟ مِنَ ٱلنَّارِ﴾

"We created not the heaven and the earth and all that is between them without purpose! That is the assumption of those who disbelieve! Then woe to those who disbelieve (in Islâmic Monotheism) from the Fire."[2]

Allâh created the creation for great wisdom and lofty purpose. He says,

﴿وَمَا خَلَقْتُ ٱلْجِنَّ وَٱلْإِنسَ إِلَّا لِيَعْبُدُونِ﴾

"And I created not the jinn and mankind except that they should worship Me."[3]

It is therefore not becoming of this All-Wise Lord to regard as equal those who obey Him and those who disobey. He says,

---

[1] Al-Hajj 22:5.
[2] Sâd 38:27.
[3] Adh-Dhâiyât 51:56.

$$\langle\!\langle \text{أَمْ نَجْعَلُ ٱلَّذِينَ ءَامَنُوا وَعَمِلُوا ٱلصَّٰلِحَٰتِ كَٱلْمُفْسِدِينَ فِى ٱلْأَرْضِ أَمْ نَجْعَلُ ٱلْمُتَّقِينَ كَٱلْفُجَّارِ} \rangle\!\rangle$$

"Shall We treat those who believe and do righteous good deeds as those who associate partners with Allâh and commit crimes on the earth? Or should We treat the pious ones as the criminals?"[1]

Therefore, it is of His Perfect Wisdom and Great Power to raise up the creation on the Day of Resurrection in order to recompense every human being for his deed; and to reward the good-doer and punish the evil doer. Allâh says,

$$\langle\!\langle \text{إِلَيْهِ مَرْجِعُكُمْ جَمِيعًا وَعْدَ ٱللَّهِ حَقًّا إِنَّهُ يَبْدَؤُا ٱلْخَلْقَ ثُمَّ يُعِيدُهُ لِيَجْزِىَ ٱلَّذِينَ ءَامَنُوا وَعَمِلُوا ٱلصَّٰلِحَٰتِ بِٱلْقِسْطِ وَٱلَّذِينَ كَفَرُوا لَهُمْ شَرَابٌ مِّنْ حَمِيمٍ وَعَذَابٌ أَلِيمٌ بِمَا كَانُوا يَكْفُرُونَ} \rangle\!\rangle$$

"To Him is the return of all of you. The promise of Allâh is true. It is He Who produced the creation and then will reproduce it, that He may reward with justice those who believed and did righteous deeds. But those who disbelieved will have a drink of boiling fluids and painful torment because they used to disbelieve."[2]

Belief in the Last Day - the Day of Resurrection - has great impacts on individuals and the society. Among its impacts are:

1. It makes man endeavour to obey Allâh seeking for

---

[1] Sâd 38:28.

[2] Yûnus 10:4. For all that has been previously mentioned, *Al-Fawaaid* by Ibn al-Qayyim p. 6, 9; and *At-Tafseer Al-Kabeer* by Ar-Raazee Vol. 2, p. 113-116.

reward of that Day and keeps him from disobeying Him out of fear of the punishment of that Day.

2. Belief in the Last Day consoles the believer on the bliss and pleasure of this world that he misses with the pleasure and reward of the Hereafter which he hopes for.

3. It is through the belief in the Last Day that man knows his fate after death and knows that he will get good reward for his deed if it is good, and get punished if it is evil. He knows that he will be made to stand for reckoning; that revenge will be taken on him for those he wronged in this world and the rights of those he wronged or oppressed would be taken back from him.

4. Belief in the Last Day actualises peace and security for mankind especially in this time that there is inadequate security and wars rage with no end - because, belief in Allâh and the Last Day makes man abstain from doing evil to others privately and publicly. That belief even penetrates his heart and makes him dismiss evil intentions -if he has any.

5. Belief in the Last Day deters man from doing injustice to others and violating their rights. If people believe in the Last Day, they will be safe from wronging one another and their rights will be protected.

6. Belief in the Last Day makes man look at this worldly abode as just one of the stages of life and that it is not the real life in itself.

To conclude this section, let us quote the words of

"Win Bet" the American Christian who used to work in one of the churches and then embraced Islâm and found the fruit of belief in the Last Day. He says, "I now know answers to the questions that had very much occupied my life. The questions are: Who am I? What do I want? Why did I come to this world? And what is my destination?"[1]

---

[1] *Ad-Da'awah Magazine* No. 1722, 19-9-1420 p. 37.

Fundamentals of the Messenger's Mission

All Prophets and Messengers were unanimous in their call to general fundamentals[1] like belief in Allâh, His angles, His Books, His Messengers; belief in the Last Day and in pre-decree, its good and bad; and like command to worship Allâh alone without ascribing any partner to Him, to follow His path and not to follow dissenting paths; like prohibiting the four kinds of sins: all evil deeds, the apparent and the hidden; sins; unjust oppression; associating partners with Allâh in worship and worshipping idols. They also agreed on deeming Allâh far from having a wife, children, associate or equal as they agreed on prohibition of saying about Him what is not true; on prohibition of infanticide, killing unjustly; eating usury; usurping of orphan's wealth. They were unanimous on enjoining the fulfilment of covenants and giving full scale and weight, being dutiful to parents; doing justice between people; being truthful in sayings and deeds; prohibition of squandering and arrogance as well as eating up people's wealth unjustly.

Ibn Al-Qayyim[2] said, "All Divine Laws are

---

[1] These general fundamentals are indicated in Suratul Baqarah 2:285, 286; and Al-An'âm 6:151, 153; Al-A'râf 7:33; Al-Isrâ 17:23, 37.

[2] His name is Muhammad bin Abee Bakr bin Ayyoob Az-Zar'ee. He was born in 691 A.H. and died in 751 A.H.. He was one of the great Islâmic scholars and he authored many great books.

unanimous in their fundamentals - even if they differ
in any other things. The goodness of these laws are
firmly rooted in the human intellect and had the laws
not come in this form, they would have been unwise,
unbeneficial and merciless though it is impossible that
they should come in any other form. Allâh says,

﴿وَلَوِ ٱتَّبَعَ ٱلْحَقُّ أَهْوَآءَهُمْ لَفَسَدَتِ ٱلسَّمَـٰوَٰتُ وَٱلْأَرْضُ وَمَن فِيهِنَّ﴾

*"And if the truth would have been in accordance with
their desires, verily, the heavens and the earth, and
whosoever is therein would have been corrupted."*[1]

How can a wise man deem it permissible that the Law
of Allâh Who is the Best of judges should come in a
form different from its present form?[2] "

This is why that all Prophets practiced one religion as
confirmed by Allâh when He says,

﴿يَـٰٓأَيُّهَا ٱلرُّسُلُ كُلُوا۟ مِنَ ٱلطَّيِّبَـٰتِ وَٱعْمَلُوا۟ صَـٰلِحًا إِنِّى بِمَا تَعْمَلُونَ عَلِيمٌ
٥١ وَإِنَّ هَـٰذِهِۦٓ أُمَّتُكُمْ أُمَّةً وَٰحِدَةً وَأَنَا۠ رَبُّكُمْ فَٱتَّقُونِ ٥٢﴾

*"O (you) Messengers! Eat of the food that Allâh has
made lawful and do righteous deeds. Verily, I am
Well-Acquainted with what you do. And verily, this
your religion (of Islâmic Monotheism) is one religion
and I am your Lord, so keep your duty to Me."*[3]

He also says,

---

[1] Al-Mu'minoon 23:71.

[2] *Miftaahu daaris-sa'aadah* Vol. 2, p. 383. See also: *Al-Jawaabus-saheeh* Vol. 4 p. 322; *Lawaami'ul-anwaar* by As-Safaareenee Vol. 2, p. 263.

[3] Al- Mu'minoon 23:51-52.

﴿شَرَعَ لَكُم مِّنَ ٱلدِّينِ مَا وَصَّىٰ بِهِۦ نُوحًا وَٱلَّذِىٓ أَوْحَيْنَآ إِلَيْكَ وَمَا وَصَّيْنَا بِهِۦٓ إِبْرَٰهِيمَ وَمُوسَىٰ وَعِيسَىٰٓ أَنْ أَقِيمُوا۟ ٱلدِّينَ وَلَا تَتَفَرَّقُوا۟ فِيهِ كَبُرَ عَلَى ٱلْمُشْرِكِينَ مَا تَدْعُوهُمْ إِلَيْهِ ٱللَّهُ يَجْتَبِىٓ إِلَيْهِ مَن يَشَآءُ وَيَهْدِىٓ إِلَيْهِ مَن يُنِيبُ﴾

"He (Allâh) has ordained for you the same religion (Islâmic Monotheism) which He ordained for Nûh (Noah) and that which We have revealed to you (O Muhammad ﷺ) and that which We ordained for Ibrâhîm (Abraham), Mûsâ (Moses) and 'Îsâ (Jesus), saying: you should establish religion (i.e., to do what it orders you to do practically). And make no divisions in it."[1]

The purpose of religion is to make mankind attain what they are created for: to worship their Lord alone without associating any partner with Him.[2] He ordained for them rites which they must fulfil and guaranteed for them obligations. He also gave them means that can make them attain that good, so that they can achieve the pleasure of their Lord and happiness in this world and the Hereafter according to a Divine Way that does not tear up man or afflict his person with deadly diseases that can cause a clash between his nature and soul and the world around him.

All Messengers called to the Divine Religion that presents man with creedal foundation in which he should believe, and the law which he should follow in his life. That is why Torah was a creed as well as a law

---

[1] Ash-Shûrâ' 42:13.
[2] *Majmoo' Fataawaa* Vol. 2, p.6.

and its followers were required to make it judge between them. Allâh says,

$$﴿إِنَّآ أَنزَلۡنَا ٱلتَّوۡرَٮٰةَ فِيهَا هُدٗى وَنُورٞ يَحۡكُمُ بِهَا ٱلنَّبِيُّونَ ٱلَّذِينَ أَسۡلَمُواْ لِلَّذِينَ هَادُواْ وَٱلرَّبَّـٰنِيُّونَ وَٱلۡأَحۡبَارُ﴾$$

"Verily, We did send down the Taurât (Torah), therein was guidance and light, by which the Prophets who submitted themselves to Allâh's Will judged for the Jews and the rabbis and the priests."[1]

Then came the Christ who brought with him the Gospel in which there was guidance and light and in confirmation of the Torah that preceded it. Allâh says,

$$﴿وَقَفَّيۡنَا عَلَىٰٓ ءَاثَـٰرِهِم بِعِيسَى ٱبۡنِ مَرۡيَمَ مُصَدِّقٗا لِّمَا بَيۡنَ يَدَيۡهِ مِنَ ٱلتَّوۡرَٮٰةِ وَءَاتَيۡنَـٰهُ ٱلۡإِنجِيلَ فِيهِ هُدٗى وَنُورٞ﴾$$

"And in their footsteps We sent 'Îsâ (Jesus) son of Mary, confirming the Torah that had come before him, and We gave him the Injeel (Gospel) in which there was guidance and light."[2]

Then Muhammad came with the final Divine Law and the complete religion as a witness over the laws that had come before it and to abrogate them. Allâh gave him the Qur'ân as a confirmation of the Divine Books that had come before it. Allâh says,

$$﴿وَأَنزَلۡنَآ إِلَيۡكَ ٱلۡكِتَـٰبَ بِٱلۡحَقِّ مُصَدِّقٗا لِّمَا بَيۡنَ يَدَيۡهِ مِنَ ٱلۡكِتَـٰبِ وَمُهَيۡمِنًا عَلَيۡهِۖ فَٱحۡكُم بَيۡنَهُم بِمَآ أَنزَلَ ٱللَّهُۖ وَلَا تَتَّبِعۡ أَهۡوَآءَهُمۡ عَمَّا جَآءَكَ مِنَ ٱلۡحَقِّ﴾$$

---

[1] Al-Mâ'idah 5:44.
[2] Al-Mâ'idah 5:46.

*"And We have sent down to you (O Muhammad ﷺ)
the Book (this Qur'ân) in truth confirming the
Scripture that came before it and a watcher over it
(old Scriptures). So judge among them by what Allâh
has revealed, and follow not their vain desires,
diverging away from the truth that has come to
you."[1]*

Allâh also explains that Muhammad and the believers
who were with him believe in Him as all Prophets
who were before them had done. He says,

﴿ءَامَنَ ٱلرَّسُولُ بِمَا أُنزِلَ إِلَيْهِ مِن رَّبِّهِۦ وَٱلْمُؤْمِنُونَ كُلٌّ ءَامَنَ بِٱللَّهِ
وَمَلَٰٓئِكَتِهِۦ وَكُتُبِهِۦ وَرُسُلِهِۦ لَا نُفَرِّقُ بَيْنَ أَحَدٍ مِّن رُّسُلِهِۦ وَقَالُوا۟
سَمِعْنَا وَأَطَعْنَا غُفْرَانَكَ رَبَّنَا وَإِلَيْكَ ٱلْمَصِيرُ﴾

*"The Messenger (Muhammad ﷺ) believes in what
has been sent down to him from his Lord and (so do)
the believers. Each one believes in Allâh, His angels,
His Books and His Messengers. They say: We make no
distinction between one another of His Messengers.
And they say: We hear and obey. (We seek) Your
Forgiveness, our Lord and to you is the return."[2]*

---

[1] Al-Mâ'idah 5:48.
[2] Al-Baqarah 2:285.

The Everlasting Message[1]

All that has been previously explained of the conditions of Judaism, Christianity, Mazdaism, Zaradashtiyah shows the situation of mankind[2] in the 6th century A.D. when the religion became corrupted and all political, social and economical conditions were also corrupted; at a time when bloody wars became widespread, dictatorship emerged and mankind lived in stark darkness. This situation led to the darkness of the hearts as a result of disbelief and ignorance. Morals became degenerated, honours and rights were violated and mischief became the order of the day in the land and on the sea. The situation was so terrible that if any wise man were to ponder over it, he would have realised that mankind - in that age - were dying and that they were heading for abyss of no return had Allâh not rescued them with a great reformer who was bearing the torch of Prophethood and the light of guidance in order to illuminate the way for mankind and guided them to the Straight Path.

At that time, Allâh permitted that the everlasting light of Prophethood should emanate from Makkah in which there is the Great House. The Makkan environment had been like other human environments in terms of polytheism, ignorance, injustice and autocracy except that it was

---

[1] For detailed reading see: *Ar-Raheequl-Makhtoom* by Safiur-Rahman Mubarakpuri

[2] See section: 'Condition of the existing religions' in this book.

distinguished from other places with many qualities some of which were:

1. It was a pure environment that had not been affected by the stains of Greek, Roman or Indian philosophy. Its natives used to enjoy deep-rooted eloquence, lively minds and exceptional dispositions.

2. It is situated in the heart of the world. It is in the middle place between Europe, Asia and Africa, an important factor that makes it easy for the ever-lasting message to spread quickly and reach these continents in a short period.

3. It is a secured place. Allâh protected it when Abraha (the Abyssinian King) wanted to invade it. The neighbouring Roman and Persian empires also were unable to conquer it. Even its commerce was secured in the north and south. That was a herald for the advent of this Noble Prophet. Allâh has reminded the inhabitants of this city of this great favour when He says,

$$\text{﴿أَوَلَمْ نُمَكِّن لَّهُمْ حَرَمًا ءَامِنًا يُجْبَىٰ إِلَيْهِ ثَمَرَٰتُ كُلِّ شَىْءٍ﴾}$$

"Have We not established for them a secured sanctuary (Makkah) to which are brought fruits of all kinds?"[1]

4. It is a desert environment that has preserved many of her good and commendable traits like generosity, good neighbourliness, earnest concern for honour among other qualities that qualified her for being the best suitable place for the clan of

---

[1] Al-Qasas 28:57.

Quraysh which was well known for eloquence, oratory and honourable traits and held the positions of honour and leadership. Allâh chose His Prophet Muhammad to make him the last of all Prophets and Messengers. He was born in Makkah in the 6th century A.D. approximately in the year 570. He grew up an orphan, for his father died while he was still in the womb. His mother and paternal grandfather later died while he was six years old. So, his uncle took care of him and he grew up an orphan. Signs of extraordinary brilliance manifested on him; and his habits, manners and traits were different from those of his people. He never lied in his speech and never hurt anyone. He became popular with truthfulness, chastity and sincerity so much so that many of his people would entrust him with their valuable properties and he would keep them as he would preserve his own life and wealth. This made them confer on him the title "Al-Ameen" (the trustworthy).

He was modest and shy and never showed himself naked in front of anyone since he came of age. He was innocent and pious and felt hurt when he saw his people worshipping idols, drinking alcohol and shedding innocent blood. He related with them only in those deeds of theirs which he loved and was pleased with and kept away from them when they indulged in their shameless acts and sins. He would help the orphans and the widows and feed the hungry.

When he was close to forty years of age, he became seriously constrained and inconvenienced by the corruption that was around him and started going

for seclusion to worship his Lord and he would ask
Him guidance to the Straight Path. While he was on
this condition, one of the angels descended upon him
with a revelation from his Lord and he commanded
him to convey this religion to mankind; to call them to
the worship of Allâh alone and to shun the worship of
others besides him. Then Revelation of ordainments
and rules continued day after day and year after year
until Allâh perfected this religion for mankind and
completed His favour on them with this perfection.
After the Messenger of Allâh had fulfilled his duty,
Allâh caused him to die. He lived for sixty-three years;
forty before prophethood and twenty-three as a
Prophet and Messenger.

Whoever ponders over the conditions of the Prophets
and studies their history will know with certainty that
there was no way in which the Prophethood of any
Prophet was established except that the Prophethood
of Muhammad was established in that way the more.
If you reflect on how the Prophethood of Moses and
'Îsâ was transmitted, you will know that it was
transmitted in succession. But the succession in
which the Prophethood of Muhammad was
transmitted was greater, stronger and more recent.
Likewise, the succession in which their miracles are
transmitted were similar but that with which the
miracles of Muhammad were transmitted is greater,
for his miracles are many and the greatest of that is the
Glorious Qur'ân which is continued to be transmitted
successively in voice and in letter.[1]

---

[1] See special section about the Qur'ân in this book. p. 153

Whoever makes a comparison between what Prophets Moses and 'Îsâ brought and what was brought by Prophet Muhammad of sound belief, wise ordainments and useful knowledge, will know with certainty that all of them emanated from a single lamp: the lamp of Prophethood. Whoever compares between the conditions of the followers of the Prophets and followers of Muhammad will know with certainty that the followers of Muhammad were the best of all people and the most of the Prophets' followers in impact on those who came after them. They have spread the Islâmic Monotheism, propagated justice and were merciful to the weak and destitute.[1]

If you want additional evidences of Muhammad's Prophethood, I will quote to you the proofs and signs that were found by 'Alee bin Rabban at-Tabaree when he was a Christian. He later embraced Islâm because of those signs. They are:

1. The Messenger called to the worship of Allâh alone and shunning the worship of others beside Him. In this, he agreed with all other Prophets.

2. He showed clear signs which only Prophets of Allâh can show.

3. He predicted the future events and they came to pass as he had predicted.

4. He predicted the occurrence of many events of the world and its countries and these events came to pass as he had predicted.

---

[1] *Majmoo' al-Fataawaa* Vol. 4 p. 201, 211; and *Ifhaamul yahood* by Samaw'al Al-Magribi p. 58-59.

5. That the Book brought by Muhammad - the Qur'ân - is a sign of Prophethood for it is the most eloquent Book, sent down unto an illiterate man who could neither read nor write, but yet challenged the orators to produce the like thereof or the like of a Sûrah[1] in it; and because of the fact that Allâh guarantees its preservation, preserved the correct belief with it, guaranteed it as the perfect divine ordainment and established with it the best community.

6. That he is the seal of all Prophets and that had he not been sent, prophecies of the past Prophets who gave glad tiding of his advent would have turned false.

7. That all Prophets had prophesied about him before his advent since a long time. They had described his mission, his country and submission of other nations and kings to him and his nation. They also mentioned the spread of his religion.

8. His victory over nations that waged war against him as a sign of his Prophethood; for it would be impossible for a man who falsely claims to be a Messenger of Allâh and yet be strengthened by Allâh with victory, authority, prevalence over enemies, spread of his message and abundance of his followers; for all this cannot happen except in

---

[1] Sûrah literary means degree. Islâmically, it is a section of the glorious Qur'ân that contains a group of Verses that may or may not be related in meanings. Some translators do translate it as a chapter which is quite inaccurate because a chapter is a combination of paragraphs in which related issues are discussed.

the hand of a truthful Prophet.

9. His religious rites and acts of worship, his decency,
   truthfulness, commendable character, manners and
   ordinances. All this cannot be found together
   except in a Prophet.

After mentioning these proofs, this guided man then
said, "These are illuminating traits and sufficient
proofs. Whoever is endowed with them must be a
Prophet; such a person has hit the target and
prospered; and the belief in him is mandatory.
Whoever rejects these proofs and denies them has
incurred loss in his efforts and lost his worldly life and
Hereafter."[1]

At the end of this section, I will narrate to you two
testimonies: that of the former Roman King who was a
contemporary of Prophet Muhammad ﷺ and that of
our contemporary Christian Evangelist John Saint.

The First Testimony: That of Heraclius:

Al-Bukhari reported the story of Abu Sufyan when the
Roman King called him. Abu Sufyan said that
Heraclius sent to him in the company of some
Qurayshi riders who went to Syria for commerce, at
a time that the Messenger of Allâh was in a truce with
Abu Sufyan and Quraysh pagans. They came to
Heraclius while they were at Ilya.[2] Heraclius
invited him to his court and with him were great

---

[1] *Ad-deen wad-dawla fee ithbaati nubuwwati Muhammad*, by 'Alee
bin Rabban At-Tabaranee p. 47. Also see: *Al-Islâm* by Al-
Qurtubee p. 362.

[2] A town in Syria.

men of Rome. He called them and his interpreter.

He then asked Abu Sufyaan and his company: "Which one of you is closest to this man who claims to be a Prophet?"

Abu Sufyan said, "I am the closest to him in blood."

Heraclius then told his retinue, "Bring him close to me and let his companions stand behind him." He then told his interpreter, "Tell them: I will ask this (Abu Sufyan) about the man who claims to be a Prophet, so, if he lies to me, you should refute that."

Abu Sufyan said, "By Allâh! If not because of the shame of having a lie being recorded against me, I would have lied about him. The first question he asked me about him was: How is his lineage amongst you?" Abu Sufyan answered, "He is of noble lineage among us."

He then asked, "Has anybody among you ever uttered this word before him?"

I said, "No."

He said, "Had anyone among his forefathers been a king?"

I said, "No."

He said, "Are his followers noble men or weak people?"

I said, "Weak people."

He said, "Do they increase or decrease?"

I said, "They increase."

He said, "Did any of them apostatised from his religion in annoyance after having embraced it?"

I said, "No"

He said, "Does he betray?"

I said, "No. But we are now in a truce with him and we do not know what he is going to do."

Abu Sufyan added, "This is the only statement I could say against him."

Heraclius further asked, "Did you go to war with him?"

I said, "Yes!"

He said, "How was your war with him?"

I said, "It was an alternate victory. He won sometimes and we won sometimes."

He said, "What does he command you to do?"

I said, "He said, 'Worship God alone and do not associate anything in worship with Him and shun what your fathers say.' He enjoined on us prayer, truthfulness, probity and kindness to the kith and kin."

Heraclius then told his interpreter, "Tell him:

I asked you of his lineage and you said that he has a noble lineage among you. That is the case with the Messengers. They were sent from the noble lineage among their people.

I asked you: Had anybody among you claimed what

he claims and you said, No. And I say: If anyone had said before him what he says now, I would have said that, he was repeating what others have said before him.

I asked you: Had any of his ancestors been a king? And you said, No. If any of his forefathers had been a king, I would have said that he is asking for the Kingdom of his father.

I asked you: Have you ever suspected him of telling lies before he said what he said and you answered, No. I then know that he could not have shunned lying to people and tell lie against God.

I asked you whether those who follow him are noble men or weak people, and you answered that his followers are weak people. Yes, those are the followers of the Messengers.

I asked you if they increase or decrease in number and you said that they increase. That is how faith does until it becomes completed.

I asked you, if any of his followers apostate in annoyance after having embraced his religion and you said, No. Yes, that is how faith does after having penetrated the hearts.

I asked you if he betray and you said, No. That is how Messengers do. They do not betray.

And I asked you about what he commanded you to do and you said that, he enjoined that you worship Allâh alone and associate nothing with Him in worship, that he enjoined on you prayers, truthfulness, chastity; that he forbids you from worshipping idols. If all that you told me is true, he shall control where I am standing now. I know that such a Prophet will emerge but I did not think that he would be from amongst you. Had I known that I would meet him, I would have suffered hardship to meet him. And had I been with him, I would have washed his feet."

He then called for the letter of the Messenger of Allâh which he sent with Dihya to the ruler of Busra. He presented the letter to Heraclius and he read it. There was in the letter;

In the Name of God, Most Gracious, Most Merciful. From Muhammad, the Messenger of Allâh, to Heraclius, the ruler of Rome. Peace be upon him who follows the guidance. I am inviting you with the invitation of Islâm. Accept Islâm, you will be safe and Allâh will give you your reward twice. But if you turn away, you will bear the sins of *Yarisin*.

﴿قُلْ يَٰٓأَهْلَ ٱلْكِتَٰبِ تَعَالَوْا۟ إِلَىٰ كَلِمَةٍ سَوَآءٍ بَيْنَنَا وَبَيْنَكُمْ أَلَّا نَعْبُدَ إِلَّا ٱللَّهَ وَلَا نُشْرِكَ بِهِۦ شَيْـًٔا وَلَا يَتَّخِذَ بَعْضُنَا بَعْضًا أَرْبَابًا مِّن دُونِ ٱللَّهِ فَإِن تَوَلَّوْا۟ فَقُولُوا۟ ٱشْهَدُوا۟ بِأَنَّا مُسْلِمُونَ﴾

"O people of the Scripture! Come to a word that is just between us and you, that we worship none but Allâh (alone) and that we associate no partner with Him, and that none of us shall take others as lords besides Allâh. Then, if they turn away, say: Bear witness that we are Muslims."[1] [Al-Imrân (3):64]

---

[1] Al-Bukhâri, the book of beginning of revelation.

The Second Testimony:

That of the contemporary Christian Evangelist John Saint who said, "After continuous reading about Islâm and its principles that serve individuals and society, and its justice in establishing a society based on foundations of equality and monotheism, I found myself embracing Islâm with all my sense and spirit and I pledged to Allâh, may He be glorified - that I would be a propagator of Islâm, and an evangelist to its guidance in all parts of the world."

This man has arrived at this certainty after having studied Christianity and beecame well-versed in it. He found that it could not provide answers to many questions of human life. So he started doubting it. Later, he studied communism and Buddhism but yet could not find what he wanted there, he finally studied Islâm deeply, then believed in it and called unto it.[1]

---

[1] *Ad-Deen Al-Fitree Al-Abadee* by Al-Mubashshir At-Taraazee Al-Husaynee 2 p. 319.

The Seal of Prophethood

It is clear to you from what he has been previously discussed, the reality of Prophethood, its signs and proofs and the signs of Prophethood of Muhammad. Before we start discussing on the seal of Prophethood, you must know that, Allâh does not send a Messenger except for one of these following reasons:

1. That the message of the Prophet is specifically meant for a particular people in which the concerned Messenger is not obliged to convey his message to the neighbouring nations, and that Allâh sends another Prophet with a special message to another nation.

2. That the message of the previous Prophet has become extinct, in which case Allâh sends another Prophet who will reform for people their religion.

3. That the Law of the previous Prophet is valid only for its time and no longer suitable for subsequent periods, then Allâh sends another Messenger with another Law that will be suitable for the another particular time and place. The Wisdom of Allâh however, has necessitated that He sends Muhammad to all mankind with a Message that is suitable for all times and places and to protect it against altering and interpolating hands, so that it can remain His Living Message by which people will live and that will be pure and free from stains of interpolations and alterations. It was for this reason

that Allâh made it the seal of all Messages.[1]

Among things with which Allâh distinguished Muhammad is that He made him the seal of all Prophets after whom there would be no Prophet. This is because, Allâh completed with him all Messages, ended with him all Laws, perfected with him the structure and actualised in his Prophethood the Prophecy of Jesus Christ when he said, ""[2]

The Reverend Ibrahîm Khaleel - who has become a Muslim - regarded this text as an equivalent of the saying of the Messenger of Allâh,

«إِنَّمَا مَثَلِي وَمَثَلُ الْأَنْبِيَاءِ، كَمَثَلِ رَجُلٍ بَنَىٰ دَارًا فَأَتَمَّهَا وَأَكْمَلَهَا إِلَّا مَوْضِعَ لَبِنَةٍ، فَجَعَلَ النَّاسُ يَدْخُلُونَهَا وَيَتَعَجَّبُونَ مِنْهَا، وَيَقُولُونَ: لَوْلَا مَوْضِعُ اللَّبِنَةِ»، قَالَ رَسُولُ اللهِ ﷺ: «فَأَنَا مَوْضِعُ اللَّبِنَةِ، جِئْتُ فَخَتَمْتُ الْأَنْبِيَاءَ عَلَيْهِمُ السَّلَامُ»

"Indeed, the example of me and that of the Prophets before me is like that of a man who has perfectly built a house and adorned it except the place of a brick in a corner which he left unfilled. People went round it and admired it and said: Why not fix up this brick? He said, 'I am the brick and I am the seal of the Prophets.'
"[3]

It is for this reason that Allâh made the Book brought by Muhammad as a witness over all previous Books

[1] *Al-Aqeedah At-Tahaawiyya* p. 156; *Lawaami'ul anwaar*, 2 p. 269, 277; and *Mabaadi'ul-Islâm* p. 64.

[2] Matthew 21:42.

[3] See, *"Muhammad in the Torah, Gospel and the Qur'ân"* by Ibrahîm Khaleel Ahmad, p. 73. The hadeeth is reported by Al-Bukhari and Muslim.

and an abolisher for them all. Just as He made the Law of Muhammad the abolisher of preceding Laws. Allâh guarantees the protection of his Message, hence, it was transmitted successfully. The Qur'ân was transmitted in succession. The practical implementation of the teachings of this religion and its acts of worship, *Sunnah* and rules were also transmitted in succession.

Whoever reads the biography of the Prophet ﷺ and his *Sunnah* will know that the Companions had preserved for humanity all situations, sayings and deeds of Muhammad ﷺ. They transmitted his acts of worship for his Lord, his strife in His cause, his remembrance of Him and his seeking for His forgiveness. They transmitted his generosity, courage, his relationship with his Companions and those visiting him. They transmitted his joy, sorrow, journeys, sojourn, manners of his eating, drinking and clothing and how he kept awake and slept. When you know all this, you will know with certainty that this religion is guaranteed by Allâh's protection and you will then know that he is the last of all Prophets and Messengers; for Allâh has told us that this Messenger is the last of all Prophets. He says,

﴿وَمَا كَانَ مُحَمَّدٌ أَبَآ أَحَدٍ مِّن رِّجَالِكُمْ وَلَكِن رَّسُولَ ٱللَّهِ وَخَاتَمَ ٱلنَّبِيِّـنَّ وَكَانَ ٱللَّهُ بِكُلِّ شَىْءٍ عَلِيمًا﴾

"Muhammad is not a father of any of your men, but he is the Messenger of Allâh and the last of the Prophets."[1]

---

[1] Al-Ahzâb 33:40.

Muhammad ﷺ also said about himself,

أُرْسِلْتُ إِلَى الْخَلْقِ كَافَّةً، وَخُتِمَ بِيَ النَّبِيُّونَ»

"I am sent to all mankind and I was made the seal of all Prophets."[1]

Now let us define Islâm and explain its essence, sources, pillars and degrees.

---

[1] Muslim :523, Ahmad 2/412..

The Meaning of the Word: Islâm

When you consult the dictionaries, you will find that the word Islâm means submission, obedience, surrender and compliance with the command and obedience of the commander without objections. Allâh has named the true religion, 'Islâm' for it is an obedience to Him, submission to His Commands without any resistance, purifying acts of worship for Him, believing in His words and having faith in Him. Islâm then became a proper name for the religion brought by Muhammad ﷺ.

Definition of Islâm

Why was this religion named Islâm? Adherents of various religions all over the world have named their religions, either with the name of a man or a particular race like Christianity, which was named after Jesus Christ; and Buddhism named after its founder Buddha; and Zaradashtism named after its founder and flag banner, Zaradasht. Judaism also emerged among the tribe of Judah and so on. It is only Islâm that is not attributed to any particular man or nation. Its name indicates a special characteristic that the meaning of Islâm denotes. It is evident in this name that no man has any role in bringing this religion into existence and that it is not peculiar with any nation to the exclusion of others. Its only goal is to make all people of the earth have characteristics of Islâm. So, whoever is characterised with the qualities of Islâm among ancient people and contemporary people is a Muslim, just as he shall be called a Muslim, anyone who possesses its qualities among the coming generations.

The Reality of Islâm

It is known that everything in this world subjects to a particular rule and established norm. The sun, the moon, the stars and the earth are all subjected to a general rule which they cannot march against or deviate from even for a hair's breadth. Even man, when you ponder over him very well, it will be clear to you that he absolutely submits to the Laws of Allâh. He cannot breath or feel a need for water, food, nourishment, light and heat except according to the Divine Decree that regulates his life; and all parts of his body submit to this Decree. The functions that these parts perform cannot be carried out except according to what Allâh has prescribed for him.

This comprehensive Divine Ordainment which man surrenders to and from which none in this universe - right from the planet in the heaven to the smallest seed in the sand of the earth - can escape from obeying is the Divine Ordainment of the Magnificent, the Sovereign and the All-Powerful Lord. If all that is in the heavens and the earth and all that is in between both surrenders to this Divine Ordainment, that means the whole world submits to and obeys that All-Powerful Sovereign Who created it. In this aspect, it is then clear that Islâm is the religion of the whole universe. For Islâm means, submission and obedience to the command of the Commander and His Prohibitions without objection as it has been previously asserted. The sun, the moon and the earth all surrender to Him. Air, water, light, darkness and heat, all surrender to Him; the tree, the stone and the animals all surrender. Even the man who does not know his Lord and denies His existence and signs or worships others besides Him, or associates others with Him in worship surrenders by nature to Him.

If you have known all that, let us now have a look at man, you will find that two factors are struggling to win his attention:

One: His natural inclination; like submission to Allâh, loving to worship Him, seeking nearness to Him, loving what He loves of truth, good and honesty; hating what He hates of falsehood, evil, injustice and wrong; and other natural factors like: love for money, family and children and desire for food, drink and sex and necessary physical functions that follow that.

Two: Man's free will and choice. Allâh has sent Messengers to him and revealed Books so that he might distinguish between truth and falsehood; guidance and error; good and evil. He gave him mental power and understanding so that he can make his choice with sure knowledge. If he so wills, he takes to the good path that leads him to truth and guidance; and if he so wills, he takes to the evil path that leads him to evil and perdition.

If you therefore, look at man in the perspective of the first factor, you will find that he is created to submit to Allâh, conditioned to adhere to that submission without making any deviation whatsoever, just like any other creature.

But if you look at him in the perspective of the second

factor, you will find him as a free creature, who chooses what he wants. He may choose to become a Muslim or to become an infidel... *"Whether he be grateful or ungrateful."*[1]

Hence, you find people divided into two categories:

A man who knows his Creator, and believes in Him as his Lord and God whom he worships alone and follows his Law in his life voluntarily. He is also conditioned to submit to his Lord, from Whom he cannot deviate and Whose ordainments he follows - such a man is the complete Muslim whose Islâm is perfect and whose knowledge is sound; for he knows Allâh, his Creator and Fashioner, Who sent Messengers to him and endowed him with the power of knowledge and learning. Such has had sound reason and correct opinion; for he has made use of his thought and then decided not to worship but Allâh Who blessed him with understanding and sound opinions in matters. His tongue speaks only the truth; for now, he only believes in One Lord Who is Allâh, the Exalted, Who gave him power to speak. It now becomes as if nothing remains in his life but the truth; for he follows and surrenders to the Law of Allâh in that which he has free will; and there exists between him and other creatures in the universe bond of familiarity and friendliness, for, he worships none but Allâh, the All-Wise, All-Knowledgeable, Whom all creatures worship, and unto Whose Commandments and Ordainments all surrender and submit. And Allâh has subjected all these creatures to you, O man!

---

[1] Al-Insân 76:3.

Reality of Disbelief

On the contrary is another man, who was born in submission to Allâh and lived all his life in submission to Allâh but never felt this submission or had any idea of it. He knew not his Lord, nor believed in His Law or followed His Messengers. He did not use the knowledge and intellect that Allâh gave him to recognize his Creator Who carved for him his ears and eyes. He rather denied His existence, he disdained His worship and refused to submit to His Laws in matters of his life in which he is given the right of disposition and choice. Or he associated others with Him in worship and refused to believe in His signs that indicate His Oneness. Such a man is a *Kaafir*. For the meaning of *'Kufr'* in the language, is 'to cover and conceal'. So this man is called a *'Kaafir'* for he conceals his nature and covers it with ignorance and insolence; and the nature of the world and that of his own self are hidden from him. You therefore, see him using his intellectual and logical power only in that which contradicts his nature. He would not see anything but that which could corrupt his nature. It is now left to you to estimate the extent of deep error and clear transgression to which the disbeliever has degenerated.[1]

This Islâm which you are required to practice is not a difficult matter, but very easy for whomsoever Allâh makes it easy for. Islâm is the religion which all this universe follow.

---

[1] *Mabaadiul Islâm* 3,4.

$$﴿وَلَهُۥٓ أَسۡلَمَ مَن فِى ٱلسَّمَٰوَٰتِ وَٱلۡأَرۡضِ طَوۡعٗا وَكَرۡهٗا وَإِلَيۡهِ يُرۡجَعُونَ﴾$$

"And to Him submitted all creatures in the heavens and the earth, willingly or unwillingly" [1]

Allâh says,

$$﴿إِنَّ ٱلدِّينَ عِندَ ٱللَّهِ ٱلۡإِسۡلَٰمُ﴾$$

"Truly, the religion with Allâh is Islâm" [2]

It is submission of one's whole self to Allâh as He, Great is His praise asserts,

$$﴿فَإِنۡ حَآجُّوكَ فَقُلۡ أَسۡلَمۡتُ وَجۡهِىَ لِلَّهِ وَمَنِ ٱتَّبَعَنِ﴾$$

"If they dispute with you (O Muhammad ﷺ) say: I have submitted to Allâh in Islâm and have those who follow me." [3]

The Messenger of Allâh ﷺ also explained the meaning of Islâm when he said,

$$﴿أَنْ تُسْلِمَ قَلْبَكَ للهِ، وَأَنْ تُوَجِّهَ وَجْهَكَ للهِ وَأَنْ تُصَلِّيَ الصَّلَاةَ الْمَكْتُوبَةَ وَتُؤَدِّيَ الزَّكَاةَ الْمَفْرُوضَةَ﴾$$

"It is to submit your heart to Allâh, to direct your face to Allâh (in worship) and to give the obligatory Zakâh." [4]

A man asked the Messenger of Allâh: 'What is Islâm?'

---

[1] Aal 'Imrân 3:83.
[2] Aal 'Imrân 3:19.
[3] Aal 'Imrân 3:20.
[4] Sahîh Ibn Hibbân Hadith no. 160, Musnad Ahmad 5/5.

«الإِسْلَامُ أَنْ يُسْلِمَ قَلْبُكَ وَأَنْ يَسْلَمَ الْمُسِلمُونَ مِنْ لِسَانِكَ وَيَدِكَ . قال : أَيُّ الإِسْلَام أَفْضَلُ؟قال : أَنْ تؤْمِنَ بِالله وَمَلْئِكَتِة وكُتُبِهِ وَرُسُلِهِ وَالْبَعْثِ بَعْدَالْمَوتِ»

The Messenger of Allâh answered: 'It is to surrender your heart to Allâh; and that Muslims should be safe from the harm of your tongue and hand.' The man said: 'Which Islâm is best?' He answered: 'The Faith (Îmân)' He asked: 'What is Faith?' He answered: 'To believe in Allâh, His angels, His Books, His Messengers and to believe in Resurrection after death.'[1]

The Messenger of Allâh also said,

«الإِسْلَامُ أَنْ تَشْهَدَ أَنْ لَا إِلَهَ إِلَّا اللهُ وَأَنَّ مُحَمَّدًا رَسُولُ الله ﷺ، وَتُقِيمَ الصَّلَاةَ، وَتُؤْتِيَ الزَّكَاةَ، وَتَصُومَ رَمَضَانَ، وَتَحُجَّ الْبَيْتَ إِنِ اسْتَطَعْتَ إِلَيْهِ سَبِيلًا»

"Islâm is to testify that there is no deity worthy of worship except Allâh and that Muhammad is the Messenger of Allâh; to observe the prayers, to give the Zakâh, to fast in the month of Ramadân and to perform pilgrimage to the House if you are able to."[2]

He also said,

«الْمُسْلِمُ مَنْ سَلِمَ الْمُسْلِمُونَ مِنْ لِسَانِهِ وَيَدِهِ»

"The Muslim is the one from the evil of whose hand

---

[1] Ahmad. See: Fadlul Islâm by Imaam Muhammad bin Abdul-Wahhaab p. 8.
[2] Muslim.

and tongue all Muslims are safe." [1]

This religion - the religion of Islâm - is the one besides which Allâh accepts no other religion, not from former generations or later generations. For all Prophets were Muslims. Allâh says about Prophet Noah,

$$﴿وَٱتۡلُ عَلَيۡهِمۡ نَبَأَ نُوحٍ إِذۡ قَالَ لِقَوۡمِهِۦ يَٰقَوۡمِ إِن كَانَ كَبُرَ عَلَيۡكُم مَّقَامِى وَتَذۡكِيرِى بِئَايَٰتِ ٱللَّهِ فَعَلَى ٱللَّهِ تَوَكَّلۡتُ إلى قوله تعالى: وَأُمِرۡتُ أَنۡ أَكُونَ مِنَ ٱلۡمُسۡلِمِينَ﴾$$

"And recite to them the news of Noah. When he said to his people: 'O my people, if my stay (with you) and my reminding you of the signs of Allâh is hard on you, then I put my trust in Allâh.'" Till He says, "...and I have been commanded to be of the Muslims." [2]

The Almighty also says about Abraham,

$$﴿إِذۡ قَالَ لَهُۥ رَبُّهُۥٓ أَسۡلِمۡۖ قَالَ أَسۡلَمۡتُ لِرَبِّ ٱلۡعَٰلَمِينَ﴾$$

"When his Lord said to him; 'Submit (i.e., be a Muslim)! He said: I have submitted myself (as a Muslim) to the Lord of all the worlds.'" [3]

He says about Moses,

$$﴿وَقَالَ مُوسَىٰ يَٰقَوۡمِ إِن كُنتُمۡ ءَامَنتُم بِٱللَّهِ فَعَلَيۡهِ تَوَكَّلُوٓاْ إِن كُنتُم مُّسۡلِمِينَ﴾$$

"And Moses said, 'O my people! If you have believed

---

[1] Al-Bukhari Hadith no.10 and Muslim Hadith no.10.
[2] Yûnus 10:71-72.
[3] Al-Baqarah 2:131

in Allâh, then put your trust in Him if you are Muslims.' "[1]

He has the following to say about Jesus Christ,

$$﴿وَإِذْ أَوْحَيْتُ إِلَى ٱلْحَوَارِيِّنَ أَنْ ءَامِنُوا بِ وَبِرَسُولِي قَالُوٓا ءَامَنَّا وَأَشْهَدْ بِأَنَّنَا مُسْلِمُونَ﴾$$

"And when I (Allâh) revealed to the disciples (of Jesus) to believe in Me and my Messenger, they said: 'We believe. And bear witness that we are Muslims.' "[2]

This religion - Islâm - derives all its laws, beliefs and rules from the Divine Revelation: the Qur'ân and Sunnah. I will give you a brief information about them.

---

[1] Yûnus 10:84.
[2] Al-Mâ'idah 5:111.

Sources of Islâm

It has been a habit for adherents of abrogated religions and man-made creeds to hallow their inherited books, which were written since ancient times and whose authors or translators or the time of their writing may not really be known. They were just written by some people who used to suffer from what other human beings suffer from like weakness, defect, whimsical desires and forgetfulness.

As for the Qur'ân, it is different from all other books in that, it depends on the true source which is the Divine Revelation: the Qur'ân and *Sunnah*. Following is the brief introduction of both:

A. The Glorious Qur'ân:

You have known previously that Islâm is the religion of Allâh, that was why Allâh revealed the Qur'ân to His Messenger, Muhammad ﷺ as a guidance for the pious, a Law for the Muslims, a healing for the disease that is in the hearts of those whom Allâh wants to heal and a light for those whom Allâh wants to give success. It contains the fundamentals for which Allâh sent the Messengers.[1] The Qur'ân was not the first Book to be revealed nor was Muhammad ﷺ the first Messenger to be sent. Allâh has revealed the Scriptures to Abraham; Torah to Moses and the Gospel to Jesus. All these Books were revelations from Allâh to His Prophets and Messengers. But the contents of most of

---

[1] *As-Sunnah wamakaanatuhaa fit-tashree'il Islâmi* by Mustafa As-Sibaa'ee p. 376.

these Books have been lost and have become extinct, and interpolation and alterations have entered them.

As for the Qur'ân, Allâh Himself guarantees its protection and makes it the witness and abolisher of earlier Books. He says while addressing the Prophet ﷺ,

﴿وَأَنزَلْنَآ إِلَيْكَ ٱلْكِتَٰبَ بِٱلْحَقِّ مُصَدِّقًا لِّمَا بَيْنَ يَدَيْهِ مِنَ ٱلْكِتَٰبِ وَمُهَيْمِنًا عَلَيْهِ﴾

"And We have sent down to you the Book (the Qur'ân) in truth, confirming the Scriptures that came before it and as a witness over it." [1]

He describes the Qur'ân as an explanation of everything,

﴿وَنَزَّلْنَا عَلَيْكَ ٱلْكِتَٰبَ تِبْيَٰنًا لِّكُلِّ شَىْءٍ﴾

"And We have sent down to you the Book as an exposition of everything." [2]

He calls it guidance and mercy,

﴿فَقَدْ جَآءَكُم بَيِّنَةٌ مِّن رَّبِّكُمْ وَهُدًى وَرَحْمَةٌ﴾

"So now has come to you a clear proof (the Qur'ân) from your Lord, and a guidance and a mercy." [3]

He describes it as that which guides to uprightness when He says,

﴿إِنَّ هَٰذَا ٱلْقُرْءَانَ يَهْدِى لِلَّتِى هِىَ أَقْوَمُ﴾

---

[1] Al-Maaidah 5:48.
[2] An-Nahl 16:89.
[3] Al-An'âm 6:157.

"Verily, this Qur'ân guides to that which is most just and right."[1]

The Qur'ân guides mankind to the most righteous path in all aspects of their life.

Whoever reflects on how the Qur'ân was revealed and how it was preserved will give the book its due estimation and purify his intention for Allâh alone. Allâh, the Exalted says,

﴿وَإِنَّهُ لَتَنزِيلُ رَبِّ ٱلْعَالَمِينَ ٠ نَزَلَ بِهِ ٱلرُّوحُ ٱلْأَمِينُ ٠ عَلَىٰ قَلْبِكَ لِتَكُونَ مِنَ ٱلْمُنذِرِينَ ٠﴾

"And truly, this (the Qur'ân) is a revelation from the Lord of all the worlds, which, the trustworthy spirit (Jibreel) has brought down upon your heart (O Muhammad ﷺ) that you may be (one) of the warners."[2]

So the One Who revealed the Qur'ân is Allâh, Lord of all the worlds; and the one who brought it is the trustworthy spirit Gabriel; and the one in whose heart it was revealed is the Prophet ﷺ.

The Qur'ân is an everlasting miracle for Muhammad ﷺ. It contains signs that shall abide till the Day of Resurrection. The signs and miracles of previous Prophets used to end at the termination of the Prophets' lives, but Allâh has made the Qur'ân the everlasting proof.

It is the extensive proof and dazzling sign. Allâh challenges the mankind to produce the like thereof or

---

[1] Al-Isrâ 17:9.
[2] Ash-Shuara26:192-194.

ten Sûrahs like it or even a single Sûrah that resembles it, and they are unable to do that in spite of the fact that it is composed of letters and words and the people on whom it was first revealed were people of eloquence and rhetoric. Allâh says,

$$﴿أَمْ يَقُولُونَ ٱفْتَرَىٰهُ قُلْ فَأْتُوا۟ بِسُورَةٍ مِّثْلِهِۦ وَٱدْعُوا۟ مَنِ ٱسْتَطَعْتُم مِّن دُونِ ٱللَّهِ إِن كُنتُمْ صَٰدِقِينَ﴾$$

"Or do they say: (Muhammad ﷺ) has forged it? Say: Bring then a Sûrah like unto it and call upon whomsoever you can besides Allâh, if you are truthful." [1]

Among the things that testify to the fact that the Qur'ân is a revelation from Allâh is that it contains stories of the past nations, prophesied future events that came to happen as it has prophesied and the fact that it mentions many scientific facts that have not been discovered until recently. Another proof of its being a Divinely revealed Book is that the Prophet on whom it was revealed was unknown with anything similar to that or reported to have known anything similar to the Qur'ân. Allâh says,

$$﴿قُل لَّوْ شَآءَ ٱللَّهُ مَا تَلَوْتُهُ عَلَيْكُمْ وَلَآ أَدْرَىٰكُم بِهِۦ فَقَدْ لَبِثْتُ فِيكُمْ عُمُرًا مِّن قَبْلِهِۦٓ أَفَلَا تَعْقِلُونَ﴾$$

"Say (O Muhammad ﷺ): If Allâh had so willed, I should not have recited it to you, nor would He have made it known to you. Verily, I have stayed amongst you a lifetime before this. Have you then no sense?" [2]

---

[1] Yûnus 10:38.
[2] Yûnus 10:16.

He was rather an illiterate who neither read nor wrote.
He did not also, visit any *Shaykh* or men to produce the
like of the Qur'ân. Allâh says,

$$﴿وَمَا كُنتَ تَتْلُواْ مِن قَبْلِهِۦ مِن كِتَٰبٍ وَلَا تَخُطُّهُۥ بِيَمِينِكَ إِذًا لَّٱرْتَابَ ٱلْمُبْطِلُونَ﴾$$

*"Neither did you (O Muhammad ﷺ) read any book
before it (the Qur'ân) nor did you write any book
(whatsoever) with your right hand. In that case,
indeed, the followers of falsehood might have
doubted."* [1]

This unlettered man who has been described in the
Torah and the Gospel that he would not read nor
write, was visited by Jewish ad Christian monks - who
had some remnants of the Torah and the Gospel - and
asked about issues by which they differed, and they
would request for his arbitration in matters in which
they contended. Allâh says, explaining the description
of Muhammad ﷺ in the Torah and the Gospel,

$$﴿ٱلَّذِينَ يَتَّبِعُونَ ٱلرَّسُولَ ٱلنَّبِيَّ ٱلْأُمِّيَّ ٱلَّذِى يَجِدُونَهُۥ مَكْتُوبًا عِندَهُمْ فِى ٱلتَّوْرَىٰةِ وَٱلْإِنجِيلِ يَأْمُرُهُم بِٱلْمَعْرُوفِ وَيَنْهَىٰهُمْ عَنِ ٱلْمُنكَرِ وَيُحِلُّ لَهُمُ ٱلطَّيِّبَٰتِ وَيُحَرِّمُ عَلَيْهِمُ ٱلْخَبَٰئِثَ﴾$$

*"Those who follow the Message, the Prophet who can
neither read nor write (i.e. Muhammad) whom they find
written with them in the Torah and the Gospel, he
commands them to do all that is good and forbids them
from all that is evil; he allows them as lawful all good
things and prohibits them as unlawful all filthy things."* [2]

---

[1] Al-'Ankabût 29:48.
[2] Al-A'râf 7:157.

Allâh also says, while speaking about the question that the Jews and Christians asked the Prophet ﷺ,

﴿يَسْـَٔلُكَ أَهْلُ ٱلْكِتَٰبِ أَن تُنَزِّلَ عَلَيْهِمْ كِتَٰبًا مِّنَ ٱلسَّمَآءِ﴾

"The People of the Scripture (Jews) ask you to cause a book to descend upon them from heaven." [1]

﴿وَيَسْـَٔلُونَكَ عَنِ ٱلرُّوحِ﴾

"And they ask you concerning the Spirit." [2]

﴿وَيَسْـَٔلُونَكَ عَن ذِى ٱلْقَرْنَيْنِ﴾

"And they ask you about Dhul-Qarnayn." [3]

﴿إِنَّ هَٰذَا ٱلْقُرْءَانَ يَقُصُّ عَلَىٰ بَنِىٓ إِسْرَٰٓءِيلَ أَكْثَرَ ٱلَّذِى هُمْ فِيهِ يَخْتَلِفُونَ﴾

"Verily, this Qur'ân narrates to the Children of Israel most of that in which they differ." [4]

Reverend Abraham Philips, has had a failed attempt, in his doctorate thesis to undermine the Qur'ân. The Qur'ân rather overwhelmed him with its proofs, evidences and signs. The man proclaimed his own weakness, surrendered to his Creator and embraced Islâm. [5]

When one of the Muslims presented a translated copy of the meaning of the Noble Qur'ân as a gift to the

---

[1] An-Nisâ' 4:153.
[2] Al-Isrâ' 17:85.
[3] Al-Kahf 18:83.
[4] An-Naml 27:76.
[5] See: *Al-Mustashriqoon wal-mubashshiroon fil-'aalamil 'arabee wal Islâmee*, Ibrahîm Khalil Ahmad.

American doctor, Jeffrey Lang, he found that this
Qur'ân was addressing him, answering his questions
and removing the barrier between him and His own
soul. He said, "It seems that He Who revealed the
Qur'ân knows me more than I know myself."[1]

Yes, the One Who revealed the Qur'ân is the Creator of
man, and He is Allâh, may He be Glorified. He says,

$$﴿أَلَا يَعْلَمُ مَنْ خَلَقَ وَهُوَ ٱللَّطِيفُ ٱلْخَبِيرُ﴾$$

*"Should not He Who has created know? And He is the
Most-Kind and Courteous, the All-Knower"* [2]

So, the man's reading of the translation of the meaning
of the Noble Qur'ân led him to Islâm and to the
writing of his book from which I am quoting.

The Qur'ân is comprehensive to all that man needs. It
contains all fundamentals of faith, legislations, human
interactions and manners. Allâh says,

$$﴿وَمَا مِن دَآبَّةٍ فِي ٱلْأَرْضِ وَلَا طَٰٓئِرٍ يَطِيرُ بِجَنَاحَيْهِ إِلَّآ أُمَمٌ أَمْثَالُكُم مَّا$$
$$فَرَّطْنَا فِي ٱلْكِتَٰبِ مِن شَيْءٍ ثُمَّ إِلَىٰ رَبِّهِمْ يُحْشَرُونَ﴾$$

"We have neglected nothing in the Book." [3]

In the Qur'ân, there is call to belief in the Oneness of
Allâh, and mention of His Names, Attributes and
deeds. It calls to belief in the authenticity of what the
Prophets and Messengers brought. It affirms the
Resurrection, reward and reckoning and establishes

---

[1] *"Struggle in the Cause of Faith"*, by Dr. Jeffrey Lang; Arabic
translation by Mundhir Al-'Absee p34.

[2] Al-Mulk 67:14.

[3] Al-An'âm 6:38.

evidences and proofs for that. It narrates the stories of past nations, the punishment meted out to them in this world as well as the torment and exemplary punishment that awaits them in the Hereafter.

It also contains many proofs and signs that dazzle the scientists and that is suitable for all generations and ages; and in which many scholars and researchers find what they look for. I will give only three examples that reveal some of these facts.

1. His saying,

﴿وَهُوَ ٱلَّذِى مَرَجَ ٱلۡبَحۡرَيۡنِ هَٰذَا عَذۡبٌ فُرَاتٌ وَهَٰذَا مِلۡحٌ أُجَاجٌ وَجَعَلَ بَيۡنَهُمَا بَرۡزَخًا وَحِجۡرًا مَّحۡجُورًا﴾

"And it is He Who has let free the seas: one palatable and sweet and the other salty and bitter; and He has set a barrier and a complete partition between them."[1]

He also says,

﴿أَوۡ كَظُلُمَٰتٍ فِى بَحۡرٍ لُّجِّىٍّ يَغۡشَٰهُ مَوۡجٌ مِّن فَوۡقِهِۦ مَوۡجٌ مِّن فَوۡقِهِۦ سَحَابٌ ظُلُمَٰتٌ بَعۡضُهَا فَوۡقَ بَعۡضٍ إِذَآ أَخۡرَجَ يَدَهُۥ لَمۡ يَكَدۡ يَرَىٰهَا وَمَن لَّمۡ يَجۡعَلِ ٱللَّهُ لَهُۥ نُورًا فَمَا لَهُۥ مِن نُّورٍ﴾

"Or is like the darkness in a vast deep sea, overwhelmed with waves topped by waves, topped by dark clouds, (layers of) darkness upon darkness: if a man stretches out his hand, he can hardly see it! And he for whom Allâh has not appointed light, for him there is no light."[2]

---

[1] Al-Furqân 25:53.
[2] An-Noor 24:40.

It is well-known that Muhammad never travelled by
sea on a sea neither was there in his time the material
instruments that could have helped to discover the
depths of the sea. Who else could have provided
Muhammad ﷺ with this data if not Allâh?

2. Allâh says,

$$﴿وَلَقَدْ خَلَقْنَا ٱلْإِنسَـٰنَ مِن سُلَـٰلَةٍ مِّن طِينٍ ○ ثُمَّ جَعَلْنَـٰهُ نُطْفَةً فِى قَرَارٍ مَّكِينٍ ○ ثُمَّ خَلَقْنَا ٱلنُّطْفَةَ عَلَقَةً فَخَلَقْنَا ٱلْعَلَقَةَ مُضْغَةً فَخَلَقْنَا ٱلْمُضْغَةَ عِظَـٰمًا فَكَسَوْنَا ٱلْعِظَـٰمَ لَحْمًا ثُمَّ أَنشَأْنَـٰهُ خَلْقًا ءَاخَرَ فَتَبَارَكَ ٱللَّهُ أَحْسَنُ ٱلْخَـٰلِقِينَ﴾$$

*"And indeed, We created man out of clay (water and
earth), therefore, We made him (the offspring of
Adam) as a mixed drops of male and female sexual
discharge (and lodged it) in a safe lodging (womb),
then We made the mixed drops into a clot (a piece of
thick coagulated blood) then We made the clot into
little lump of flesh, then we made out of that little
lump of flesh bones, then We clothed the bone with
flesh and We brought it forth as another Creation. So,
blessed is Allâh, the Best of Creators."[1]*

The scientists did not discover these subtle details
about the stages of embryonic development until
recently.

3. Allâh also says,

$$﴿وَعِندَهُۥ مَفَاتِحُ ٱلْغَيْبِ لَا يَعْلَمُهَآ إِلَّا هُوَ ۚ وَيَعْلَمُ مَا فِى ٱلْبَرِّ وَٱلْبَحْرِ ۚ وَمَا تَسْقُطُ مِن وَرَقَةٍ إِلَّا يَعْلَمُهَا وَلَا حَبَّةٍ فِى ظُلُمَـٰتِ ٱلْأَرْضِ وَلَا$$

---

[1] Al-Mu'minûn 23:12-14.

$$\text{رَطْبٍ وَلَا يَابِسٍ إِلَّا فِي كِتَابٍ مُّبِينٍ}$$

"And with Him are the keys of all that is hidden, none knows them but He. And He knows whatever there is in the land and in the sea; not a leaf falls but He knows it. There is not a grain in the darkness of the earth nor anything fresh or dry, but is written in a Clear Record." [1]

Mankind did not know this all-encompassing thought and had never thought about these things let alone having the ability to do it. If a group of scientists observe a plant or insect and they record their findings and discoveries we all become dazzled with that, though we know that what is hidden from these scientists in this plant or insect is more than what they observe in it.

The French scholar Maurice Bucaile has made a comparison between Torah, the Gospel and the Qur'ân and between modern scientific discoveries concerning the creation of the heavens, the earth and man and found out that these modern discoveries agree with what is in the Qur'ân. On the other hand, he found out that the Torah and the Gospel that are in circulation today contain many erroneous information about the creation of the heavens, the earth, man and animals. [2]

B. The Prophetic *Sunnah*:

---

[1] Al-An'âm 6:59.

[2] See: "The Torah, the Bible and the Qur'ân in the light of modern science" by Maurice Bucaile p. 133-283. He was a Christian revert.

Allâh revealed the Qur'ân to the Messenger ﷺ and revealed to him like thereof which is the Prophetic *Sunnah* that explains the Qur'ân. The Messenger of Allâh ﷺ said,

«أَلَا، إِنِّي أُوتِيتُ الْكِتَابَ وَمِثْلَهُ مَعَهُ»

"Indeed, I am given the Qur'ân and its like with it." [1]

Allâh has permitted him to explain the general and particular Verses of the Qur'ân. Allâh says,

﴿وَأَنزَلْنَآ إِلَيْكَ ٱلذِّكْرَ لِتُبَيِّنَ لِلنَّاسِ مَا نُزِّلَ إِلَيْهِمْ وَلَعَلَّهُمْ يَتَفَكَّرُونَ﴾

"And We have also sent down to you (O Muhammad ﷺ) the reminder, that you may explain clearly to men what is sent down to them, and that they may give thought." [2]

The *Sunnah* is the second source of the religion of Islâm. It means all that is reported from the Prophet - with well-connected and authentic chain of transmitters - of his sayings, deeds, confirmations and qualities. It is also a revelation from Allâh to His Messenger Muhammad ﷺ, for the Prophet did not speak of his own desire. Allâh says,

﴿وَمَا يَنطِقُ عَنِ ٱلْهَوَىٰ ٠ إِنْ هُوَ إِلَّا وَحْيٌ يُوحَىٰ ٠ عَلَّمَهُ شَدِيدُ ٱلْقُوَىٰ﴾

"Nor, does he speak of (his own) desire, it is only a Revelation revealed. He has been taught by one

---

[1] Ahmad (17174) and Abû Dawood (4604).
[2] An-Nahl 16:44.

mighty in power (Gabriel)." [1]

The Prophet only conveys to people what he is commanded to convey. Allâh says about him,

﴿إِنْ أَتَّبِعُ إِلَّا مَا يُوحَىٰ إِلَيَّ وَمَا أَنَا۟ إِلَّا نَذِيرٌ مُّبِينٌ﴾

"I only follow that which is revealed to me, and I am but a plain warner." [2]

The pure *Sunnah* is the practical implementation of the rules, beliefs, acts of worship, kinds of relationship and manners that Islâm enjoins. The Messenger of Allâh exemplified what he was commanded, explained it to the people and commanded them to do like he did. He says, for instance,

«صَلُّوا كَمَا رَأَيْتُمُونِي أُصَلِّي»

"Pray as you see me praying." [3]

The All-Mighty Allâh has commanded the believers to emulate him in all his deeds and sayings in order that their faith might be complete. He says,

﴿لَّقَدْ كَانَ لَكُمْ فِي رَسُولِ ٱللَّهِ أُسْوَةٌ حَسَنَةٌ لِّمَن كَانَ يَرْجُوا۟ ٱللَّهَ وَٱلْيَوْمَ ٱلْءَاخِرَ وَذَكَرَ ٱللَّهَ كَثِيرًا﴾

"Indeed, in the Messenger of Allâh, you have a good example to follow for him who hopes for (the meeting with) Allâh and the Last Day and remembers Allâh much." [4]

---

[1] An-Najm 53:3-5.
[2] Al-Ahqâf 46:9.
[3] Al-Bukhâri.
[4] Al-Ahzâb 33:21.

The Prophet's noble Companions transmitted his sayings and deeds to those who came after them, and these also transmitted them to those who came after them. It was then recorded in the books of *Sunnah*. The *Sunnah* transmitters had been strict with those from whom they transmitted it and would make a condition that they be contemporaries of those from whom they themselves reported that *Sunnah*, till the chain of transmission would be connected right from the narrator to the Messenger of Allâh.[1] They also made it a condition that all the men involved in the transmission must be trustworthy, just, sincere and people of integrity.

The *Sunnah*, as it is regarded as the practical implementation of Islâm, it also explains the Qur'ân, makes comments on it, and explains verses that have general meanings. The Messenger of Allâh ﷺ used to do all this, sometimes with his words, sometimes with his deeds and sometimes with both. The *Sunnah* may, in some cases, give independent explanations of some rules and legislations that are not in the Qur'ân.

One must have belief in the Qur'ân and *Sunnah* that they are the basic sources of the religion of Islâm that must be followed and turned to. The command of both must be obeyed, their prohibitions must be abstained from and their contents must be believed. One must

---

[1] As a result of this unique academic methodology and accuracy and precision in transmitting the *Sunnah*, a science was introduced among the Muslims, that are known as 'ilmul-jarh wat-ta'deel' and 'ilm mustalahul-hadeeth'. The two sciences are among the exclusive qualities of the Muslims, which none possessed before them.

also believe in what both contain of the Names, Attributes and Works of Allâh; what He has provided for His believing friends and that with which He threatened His disbelieving enemies. He says,

﴿فَلَا وَرَبِّكَ لَا يُؤْمِنُونَ حَتَّىٰ يُحَكِّمُوكَ فِيمَا شَجَرَ بَيْنَهُمْ ثُمَّ لَا يَجِدُواْ فِىٓ أَنفُسِهِمْ حَرَجًا مِّمَّا قَضَيْتَ وَيُسَلِّمُواْ تَسْلِيمًا﴾

"But no, by your Lord, they can have no faith, until they make you (O Muhammad ﷺ) judge in all disputes between them, and find in themselves no resistance against your decisions, and accept (them) with full submission."[1]

He also says,

﴿وَمَآ ءَاتَىٰكُمُ ٱلرَّسُولُ فَخُذُوهُ وَمَا نَهَىٰكُمْ عَنْهُ فَٱنتَهُواْ﴾

"And whatsoever the Messenger gives you, take it; and whatsoever he forbids you, abstain (from it)."[2]

After giving an introduction about the sources of this religion, it is appropriate for us to discuss about its degrees which are: Islâm, Imân and Ihsaan. We are also going to talk on the pillars of these degrees in brief.

---

[1] An-Nisâ' 4:65.

[2] Al-Hashr 59:7.

The First Degree[1]

Islâm: Its pillars are five, they are: Testifying that there is no deity worthy of worship but Allâh and that Muhammad is His Messenger; performing prayer, paying Zakât, fasting in the month of Ramadan and *Hajj*.

One: *Shahadah*. Testifying that there is no deity worthy of worship save Allâh and that Muhammad is His Messenger.

The first part of the testimony means that, there is no rightful deity in the earth or in the heavens beside Him alone. He is the only true God and all deities besides Him are false ones.[2] It also means, purifying all acts of worship for Allâh alone and keeping them away from others beside Him. The utterer of this statement cannot benefit from it until he has two things:

1. To say it out of belief, knowledge, conviction and love for it.

2. To disbelieve in all that is worshipped besides Allâh. Whoever says this statement and does not disbelieve in all that is worshipped besides Allâh,

---

[1] For more details see, "*Kitaabut-Tawheed*", "*Al-Usooluth-Thalaathah*", "*Aadaabul-mashyi ilas-Salaah*" by Shaykh Muhammad bin Abdul-Wahhab.
See also: "*Deenul-Haqq*" by Abdur-Rahmaan Al-Umar; "*Maalaabudda min ma'rifatihi anil Islâm*" by Muhammad bin 'Alee al-Arfaj; "*Arkaanul Islâm*" by Abdullah Al-Jaarallah; "*Sharh arkaanil Islâm wal Eemaan*" by a group of students and reviewed by Shaykh Abdullaah Al-Jibreen.

[2] *Deenul-Haqq* p. 38.

this statement will not benefit him.[1]

Testifying that Muhammad is the Messenger of Allâh means, to follow him in all that he commands, to believe in all that he informs, to abstain from all that he prohibits and warns against and to worship Allâh with only what he legislates. One must also know and bear it in mind that Muhammad is Allâh's Messenger to all people, that he is only a slave of Allâh and should therefore not be worshipped, but rather be obeyed and followed, that whoever follows him enters Paradise and whoever disobeys him enters Fire. One must also know and bear it in mind that, Islâmic injunctions in matters of belief, acts of worship which are commanded by Allâh, system of law and matters of legislation and morals in area of building a family, or in area of allowing or forbidding things cannot be received except through this noble Prophet, for he is the Messenger of Allâh, who conveys His Law to mankind.[2]

Two: Prayer.[3]

Prayer is the second pillar of Islâm. It is rather the pillar of Islâm, for it is the link between man and his Lord. He repeats it five times in a day with which he renews his faith, purifies himself from stains of sins and which stands between him and obscene things and sins. When he wakes up from sleep in the morning, he appears in front of his Lord pure and

---

[1] *Qurratu 'uyoonul muwahhideen*, p. 60.

[2] For more details, read, "*Kayfiyyatul Salaatin-Nabiyy*" by Shaykh bin Baaz.

[3] *Deenul-Haqq* p. 51-52.

clean before he starts engaging in matters of this world. He magnifies his Lord, affirms His absolute right to be worshipped by prostrating, standing and bowing for Him five times each day.

Before he starts performing this prayer, he must purify his heart, body, clothes and place of his prayer. The Muslim must perform this prayer congregationally with his fellow Muslims - if that is easy for him - while they all face their Lord with their hearts and face the honoured Ka'abah, the House of Allâh with their faces. Prayer has been prescribed in the best form in which the Creator requires His creation to worship Him; for it contains His glorification with all parts of the body; from word of the tongue, deeds of the hands, legs, head, senses and all other parts of his body; each part taking its share of this great act of worship.

The senses and limbs take their portion from it and the heart also takes its share. Prayer comprises of exaltation of Allâh, praising Him, glorifying Him, extolling Him. It also contains giving the testimony of the truth, recitation of the Qur'ân, standing in front of the Lord Who controls him, then humiliating oneself for Him in this position by begging Him with devotion and seeking His nearness. He then goes to bowing position, prostration and then sits down, all in submission, humility and showing helplessness for His greatness and His Might. The heart of this slave becomes broken, his body becomes humble and all his limbs surrender with humility to his Lord. He then concludes his prayer with giving thanks to Allâh and praising Him, and invoking peace and blessings on

His Prophet, Muhammad and finally asks his Lord of the good things of this world and the Hereafter.[1]

Three: *Zakâh*[2]

Zakâh - obligatory charity - is the third pillar of Islâm. It is compulsory on the rich Muslims to pay *Zakâh* from his wealth. It is a very little part of his wealth that he gives to the poor and needy and others among those who are entitled to it.

Muslims must pay *Zakâh* to its due recipients willingly. He should neither remind the recipient of that nor harm him in whatever way on account of it. He must pay it seeking for the pleasure of Allâh; not desiring by that any recompense or thanks from men. He should rather pay it for the sake of Allâh not for showing off or for any fame.

Paying *Zakâh* brings blessings and gladdens the hearts of the poor, the destitute and the needy. It prevents them from begging and it is a compassion on them and protection against negligence and poverty that could have afflicted them if they are left by the wealthy. Paying *Zakâh* when it is due is a quality of generosity, magnanimity, altruism, philanthropy and compassion. It also means freeing one self from traits of stingy, avaricious and valueless people. It is by *Zakâh* that Muslims support one another, that the wealthy shows mercy on the poor, so that there will not remain in the community - if this rite is properly implemented - a poor and destitute, a subdued debtor

---

[1] For more, read *"Risaalataani fiz-zakaati was-siyaam"* by Shaykh Ibn Baz.
[2] *Miftaah daar as-sa'aadah* 2:384.

or a traveller who has no more provisions with him.

Four: Fasting

It is to fast in the month of Ramadan from the dawn to the sunset. The fasting Muslim abandons food, drink, sexual intercourse and similar things as an act of worship for Allâh and curbs his own soul from fulfilling its desires. Allâh has relieved the sick, the traveller, the pregnant woman, the nursing mother and a woman who has just delivered a baby from fasting. He ordained for each of them rules that suit him or her.

In this month, a Muslim curbs his own self from his desires and this act of worship will bring his soul out of the animal-like world to the world similar to that of angels who are near to Allâh. The situation of a fasting Muslim may reach a stage that he thinks like someone who has no need in this world more than to achieve the pleasure of Allâh.

Fasting enlivens the heart, makes one renounce the world, encourages one to seek what is with Allâh, and reminds the wealthy of the poor ones and their conditions so that their hearts may have sympathy for them and know that they are living in the favour of Allâh and therefore should increase in gratitude to him.

Fasting purifies the soul and create in it the fear of Allâh. It makes individuals and the society feel the control of Allâh on them in bliss and hardship and in public and secret; where the society spends a whole month observing this act of worship and being conscious of its Lord; while being spurred by the fear of Allâh, the Exalted, by a belief that Allâh knows what is hidden and secret, that man will inevitably stand before Him a day in which He will ask him about all his deeds: minor and major.[1]

Five: *Hajj*[2]

Pilgrimage to the House of Allâh in Makkah. It is obligatory on every Muslim who is adult, sane and capable; who possesses or can afford to hire means of transportation to Makkah and also possesses what is sufficient for him to live on throughout his journey with a condition that his provision should be an excess of the provision of those who are his dependants. He should also be sure that the road is safe and must ensure security of his dependants while he is away. *Hajj* is compulsory once in the lifetime for whoever is able to perform it.

One who intends to do *Hajj* should repent to Allâh in order that his soul can be free from filth of sins. When he reaches Makkah and other holy sites, he carries out the rites of *Hajj* as an act of worship and glorification for Allâh. He must know that the Ka'bah as well as other sites should not be worshipped beside Allâh, for they neither benefit nor harm. He should also know that had Allâh not commanded the Muslims to embark on *Hajj* pilgrimage to that House, it would not have been proper for any Muslim to do that.

---

[1] See "*Miftaah daar as-sa'aadah*" 2, p. 384.

[2] For detailed reading see: "*Daleelul-Hajj wal mu'tamir*" by a group of scholars and "*Explanations in many issues pertaining to Hajj and Umrah*" by Shaykh Ibn Baz.

In *Hajj* pilgrimage, the pilgrim wears two white garments. The Muslims gather from all parts of the world at one place, wearing one garment and worshipping One God; with no difference between the leader and the led; the rich and the poor; the white and the black. All are creatures of Allâh and His slaves. There is no superiority for a Muslim over another Muslim except by piety and good deeds.

By *Hajj*, Muslims achieve cooperation and mutual recognition, they remember the Day that Allâh will raise all of them up and gather them at a single place for reckoning, they thereby prepare for what is after death through acts of obedience to Allâh.

Worship in Islâm:[1]

It is to worship Allâh in meaning and reality. Allâh is the Creator and you are the creature; you are the slave and He is the One that you worship. If that is the case, man must then follow the Straight Path of Allâh in this life and follow His Law and the Path of his Messengers. Allâh has ordained great laws for His slaves like belief in His Oneness, performing prayers, paying Zakâh, observing fasting and performing *Hajj*.

However, the above mentioned are not the only acts of worship in Islâm. Worship in Islâm is more comprehensive. It is all that Allâh loves and is pleased with deeds and sayings, apparent or hidden. So, every work or saying that you do or say that Allâh loves and He is pleased with is worship. Even, every good habit that you do with an intention to please

---

[1] See "*Al-uboodiyyah*" by Shaykhul Islâm Ibn Taymiyyah.

Allâh is worship. Your good relationship with your father, family, spouse, children and neighbours if you seek by that the pleasure of Allâh is worship. Your good conduct at home, in the market and office, done for the sake of Allâh is worship. Fulfilling the trust, being truthful and just, abstention from harming others, giving assistance to the weak, earning from lawful means, spending for family and children, consoling the poor, visiting the sick, feeding the hungry and aiding the wronged are all acts of worship if done for the sake of Allâh. So, all deeds that you do either for yourself, family or the society or your country in which you intend to win the pleasure of Allâh are acts of worship.

Even to fulfil your personal passion in a lawful way is worship if you do that with a good intention. The Messenger of Allâh ﷺ said,

«وَفِي بُضْعِ أَحَدِكُمْ صَدَقَةٌ» قَالُوا: يَا رَسُولَ اللهِ! أَيَأْتِي أَحَدُنَا شَهْوَتَهُ وَيَكُونُ لَهُ فِيهَا أَجْرٌ؟ قَالَ: «أَرَأَيْتُمْ لَوْ وَضَعَهَا فِي حَرَامٍ، أَكَانَ عَلَيْهِ فِيهَا وِزْرٌ؟ فَكَذَلِكَ إِذَا وَضَعَهَا فِي الْحَلَالِ كَانَ لَهُ أَجْرٌ»

"Even if anyone of you satiate his sexual desires, that is an act of charity. "The Companions said, "O Messenger of Allâh! Would any of us satiate his own lust and still get a reward?" He answered, "Tell me, if he had done that in an unlawful way would not he have sinned? Likewise, if he does it in a lawful way, he would get a reward." [1]

---

[1] Muslim (1006).

The Prophet ﷺ also said,

«عَلى كُلِّ مُسْلِمٍ صَدَقَةٌ». فَقَالُوا: يا نَبِيَّ اللهِ! فَمَنْ لَمْ يَجِدْ؟ قالَ: «يَعْمَلُ بِيَدِهِ فَيَنْفَعُ نَفْسَهُ وَيَتَصَدَّقُ». قالُوا: فإِنْ لَمْ يَجِدْ؟ قالَ: «يُعِينُ ذَا الحاجَةِ المَلْهُوفَ». قالُوا: فإِنْ لَمْ يَجِدْ؟ قالَ: «فَلْيَعْمَلْ بالمَعْرُوفِ وَلْيُمْسِكْ عَنِ الشَّرِّ فإِنَّها لَهُ صَدَقَةٌ»

"Every Muslim must pay charity." He was asked, *"How if he does not find what to pay charity with?"* He said, *"He works with his two hands benefits himself by that and then pay charity."* He was asked again, *"But how if he is not able?"* He said, *"He should assist the needy who is wronged."* He was again asked, *"But how if he is not able?"* He answered, *"He enjoins all that is good."* And he was asked once more, *"But how, if he is not able to do that?"* He answered, *"He refrains from doing evil, for that also is for him, an act of charity."*[1]

---

[1] Bukhâri (1445) and Muslim (1008).

The Second Degree[1]

Faith and its six pillars: Belief in Allâh, His angels, His Books, His Messengers, belief in the Last Day and belief in pre-decree.

One: Belief in Allâh.

You must believe in His Lordship; that He is the Lord, the Creator, the Possessor and the Controller of all matters. You must also believe in His right to be worshipped, that He is the only True Deity, that all deities besides Him are false. You must believe in His Names and Attributes, that He has Beautiful Names and perfect Sublime Attributes.

You must also believe in His Oneness in all that, that He has no partner in His Lordship, nor in His right to be worshipped or in His Names and Attributes. He says,

﴿رَّبُّ ٱلسَّمَٰوَٰتِ وَٱلْأَرْضِ وَمَا بَيْنَهُمَا فَٱعْبُدْهُ وَٱصْطَبِرْ لِعِبَٰدَتِهِۦ هَلْ تَعْلَمُ لَهُۥ سَمِيًّا﴾

"Lord of the heavens and the earth, and all that is between them, so worship Him and be constant and patient in His worship. Do you know of any who is similar to Him?"[2]

You must also believe that neither slumber nor sleep

---

[1] For more, read, *"Sharh usool al-eeman"* by Ibn 'Uthaymeen; *"Kitaabul eemaan"* by Ibn Taymiyyah; *"Aqeedatul ahlissunnah waljamaa'ah"* by Ibn 'Uthaymeen.

[2] Maryam 19:65.

overtakes Him; that He knows all that is hidden and evident; and that to him belongs the sovereignty of the heavens and the earth. He says,

﴿وَعِندَهُۥ مَفَاتِحُ ٱلْغَيْبِ لَا يَعْلَمُهَآ إِلَّا هُوَ وَيَعْلَمُ مَا فِى ٱلْبَرِّ وَٱلْبَحْرِ وَمَا تَسْقُطُ مِن وَرَقَةٍ إِلَّا يَعْلَمُهَا وَلَا حَبَّةٍ فِى ظُلُمَٰتِ ٱلْأَرْضِ وَلَا رَطْبٍ وَلَا يَابِسٍ إِلَّا فِى كِتَٰبٍ مُّبِينٍ﴾

"And with Him are the keys of all that is hidden, none knows them but He. And He knows whatever is in the land and in the sea; not a leaf falls but He knows it. There is not a grain in the darkness of the earth nor anything fresh or dry, but is written in a Clear Record."[1]

You must also believe that He - may He be exalted - rose high over His Throne above His creation, and that He is with them by His knowledge and He knows their conditions, hears their utterances, sees their places and controls their affairs. He provides for the poor, gives relief to the dejected, gives authority to whom He wills, withdraws it from whom He wills and that He is Able to do all things.[2]

Among the benefits of belief in Allâh are the following:

1. It lets man love Allâh and glorify Him and as such carry out His commandments and abstain from all that He forbids. If man does that, he attains perfect happiness in this world and the Hereafter.

2. Belief in Allâh creates in the mind self-esteem and dignity, for through it, man will know that it is only

---

[1] Al-An'âm 6:59.
[2] See: " 'Aqeedatul ahlissunnah waljamaa'ah " p. 7, 11.

Allâh who is the True Possessor of all that is in this universe, that there is no bringer of harm or benefit except Him. This knowledge makes him dispenses of all that is besides Allâh and removes from his heart the fear of others besides Allâh and he will not hope except for Allâh and will not fear except Him alone.

3. Belief in Allâh creates humbleness in the heart; for man will know that whatever favour he has is from Allâh. Satan will not be able to deceive him, nor will he become overbearing and arrogant or boast with his power or wealth.

4. The believer in Allâh will have certain knowledge that there is no way to success and salvation except through good deeds that please Allâh. Some people, however have false belief that Allâh commanded that His son be crucified as an atonement for the sins of mankind; some have a belief in false deities believing that these will do for them what they want while actually they can neither benefit nor harm; while some are atheists, who do not believe in the existence of Creator at all. All these beliefs are mere wishful thoughts; for when those who hold these beliefs meet Allâh on the Day of Resurrection and they see the reality, they will realise that they have been in clear error.

5. Belief in Allâh creates in man great power of determination, courage, perseverance, steadfast-ness and trust in Allâh when he struggles in lofty matters in this world to achieve the pleasure of Allâh. He will be on perfect certainty that he is

putting his trust in the Possessor of the heavens and the earth and that He will help him and guide him. He will then be firm like mountains in his patience, steadfastness and in his trust in Allâh.[1]

Two: Belief in the Angels.

﴿وَقَالُوا اتَّخَذَ الرَّحْمَنُ وَلَدًا سُبْحَانَهُ بَلْ عِبَادٌ مُّكْرَمُونَ ۝ لَا يَسْبِقُونَهُ بِالْقَوْلِ وَهُم بِأَمْرِهِ يَعْمَلُونَ ۝ يَعْلَمُ مَا بَيْنَ أَيْدِيهِمْ وَمَا خَلْفَهُمْ وَلَا يَشْفَعُونَ إِلَّا لِمَنِ ارْتَضَى وَهُم مِّنْ خَشْيَتِهِ مُشْفِقُونَ﴾

And they say: "The Most Gracious (Allâh) has begotten a son (or children)." Glory to Him! They [whom they call children of Allâh i.e. angels, are but honoured slaves. They speak not until He has spoken and they act on His Command. He knows what is before them and what is behind them, and they cannot intercede except for him with Whom He is pleased and they stand in awe for fear of Him."[2]

He also described them that,

﴿وَلَهُ مَن فِي السَّمَاوَاتِ وَالْأَرْضِ وَمَنْ عِندَهُ لَا يَسْتَكْبِرُونَ عَنْ عِبَادَتِهِ وَلَا يَسْتَحْسِرُونَ ۝ يُسَبِّحُونَ اللَّيْلَ وَالنَّهَارَ لَا يَفْتُرُونَ﴾

They, "are not too proud to worship Him, nor are weary (of His worship). They glorify His praises night and day (and) they never slacken (to do so)."[3]

Allâh conceals them from our eyes, so that we do not see them. But Allâh sometimes shows some of them to

---

[1] See: 'Aqeedatul ahlissunnah waljamaa'ah p. 44 and *Mabadiul Islâm* p. 80, 84.

[2] Al-Anbiyâ' 21:26-28.

[3] Al-Anbiyâ' 21:19-20.

some of His Prophets and Messengers.

Angels have functions assigned to them. Jibreel is assigned to Revelations which he brings from Allâh to whosoever He wishes of His Messengers. Among them is also an angel assigned to taking the souls, among them are those assigned to the foetuses in the wombs, among them are those assigned to the protection of mankind and among them are those assigned to recording of their deeds. Every person has two angels

$$﴿ إِذْ يَتَلَقَّى ٱلْمُتَلَقِّيَانِ عَنِ ٱلْيَمِينِ وَعَنِ ٱلشِّمَالِ قَعِيدٌ ۝ مَّا يَلْفِظُ مِن قَوْلٍ إِلَّا لَدَيْهِ رَقِيبٌ عَتِيدٌ ﴾$$

"one sitting on the right and one on the left (to note his or her actions) not a word does he (or she) utter but there is a watcher by him (or her) ready (to record it)"[1]

Benefits of Belief in Angels

1. It purifies the belief of the Muslim from stains of polytheism; for when a Muslim believes in the existence of angels whom Allâh assigns with these great functions, he will be free from belief in the existence of imaginary creatures that some people claim have a share in the running of the affairs of the universe.

2. It lets the Muslims know that, the angels neither benefit nor harm, but that they are honoured slaves, who disobey not Allâh when He commands

---
[1] Qâf 50:17-18.

them but rather do what they are commanded. He
will not worship them, nor direct his affairs to them
or depend on them.

Three: Belief in the Books

To believe that Allâh revealed Books to his Prophets
and Messengers, in order to explain the truth and call
to it. Allâh says,

$$﴿لَقَدْ أَرْسَلْنَا رُسُلَنَا بِٱلْبَيِّنَٰتِ وَأَنزَلْنَا مَعَهُمُ ٱلْكِتَٰبَ وَٱلْمِيزَانَ لِيَقُومَ ٱلنَّاسُ بِٱلْقِسْطِ﴾$$

*"Indeed, We have sent Our Messengers with clear
proofs, and revealed with them the Scripture and the
Balance (justice), that mankind may keep up
justice."*[1]

These Books are many. Among them are the Scripture
of Prophet Ibrahîm, the Torah of Prophet Mûsâ, the
Psalms given to Prophet David and the Gospel which
was brought by Prophet Jesus Christ, may peace be
upon all of them.

Belief in the Previous Books lies in believing that it is
Allâh Who revealed them to His Messengers and that
they contained the Law that Allâh wanted to be
conveyed to people at that time.

All these Books that Allâh informs us about have all
become extinct. The scripture of Abraham is no longer
existing in the world. As for the Torah, the Gospel and
the Psalms, even though they do exist by name in the
hands of Jews and Christians, they have become

---

[1] Al-Hadeed 57:25.

altered, interpolated and adulterated and many of their original contents are missing. That which are not part of them have been included in them, and they are attributed to those who are not their authors. The old testament for instance, has more than forty books, and only five of them were attributed to Moses. As for the existing gospels of today, nothing of them is attributed to Jesus. The last Book revealed by Allâh is the Qur'ân which was revealed to Prophet Muhammad ﷺ. It has always been and still is protected and preserved by Allâh. No change or alteration has crept into any of its letters, words, vowels or meanings.

The Qur'ân is different from all previous Books in many ways:

1. The past Books have been lost; changes and interpolations have crept into them; they have been attributed to those who are not their rightful owners; many commentaries and exegesis have been added to them and they contain many things that contradict Divine Revelation, the reason and nature. As for the Qur'ân, it is still being protected by Allâh, with its letters and words in which Allâh revealed them to Muhammad. No alteration nor addition has crept into it; for Muslims have been eager to let the Qur'ân remain free from all defects. They do not mix it with anything from the Prophet's life history, or the history of his Companions or commentaries of the Qur'ân or rules pertaining to acts of worship and human relations.

2. Today, there is no known historical authority for the ancient books. Even, nothing was known about

those on whom some of them were revealed or in
which language they were revealed. Some of them
are even attributed to others beside those who
actually brought them.

As for the Qur'ân, Muslims have transmitted it from
Muhammad ﷺ in a successive manner, verbally and
in written form. And at every age and country, there
are thousands of Muslims who know this Book by
heart as there are thousands of its copies as well. If the
oral copies do not agree with written copies, the
divergent copies will not be recognised; for what is in
the memories of people should always be in
agreement with what is in the written copies.

Above all, the Qur'ân was transmitted orally in a way
that nothing of the books of this world had enjoyed.
Even this particular method of transmission cannot be
found except among Muslims alone. The methodology
of preserving the Qur'ân goes this way: The student
learns the Qur'ân by heart at the hand of his teacher;
who had in turn learnt it by heart at the hand of his
own teacher. The teacher also gives the student a
certificate called "Ijaazah" in which the teacher testifies
that he taught the student what he himself learnt from
his own teachers one after another, each and everyone
of these teachers will name his teacher from whom he
learnt the Qur'ân in succession till the chain reaches
the Messenger of Allâh himself. This is how the chain
of teachers go in oral succession till it reaches the
Messenger of Allâh ﷺ.

There exists many strong evidences and historical
proofs - with connected chains of transmitters - on the

knowledge of every Sûrah and every Verse of the
Qur'ân as regards where it was revealed and when it
was revealed to Muhammad ﷺ.

3. The languages in which past Books were revealed
   had become extinct since a long time. No one in this
   age speaks the languages and very few people can
   now understand them. As for the language in
   which the Qur'ân was revealed, it is a living
   language spoken today by tens of millions of
   people. It is taught and studied in every country
   of the world. Even the one who does not study it
   will find everywhere those who can teach him the
   meaning of the Qur'ân.

4. Each of the previous Books was meant for a
   particular time and sent to a particular nation; that
   was why it contained rules that were peculiar to
   that nation and that time. Whatever book that has
   these characteristics is not suitable for all mankind.

   As for the Great Qur'ân, it is a Book meant for all
   times and all places. It comprises of ordainments,
   rules on how humans should relate with one
   another and manners that are suitable for every
   age; for it is addressed to mankind in general.

In view of the above, it becomes clear that it is not
possible that Allâh's proof against humanity should be
in books whose original copies no longer exist and
whose languages no one in the world of today speaks,
after they have been altered. Allâh's proof against His
creation should be in a Book, protected and safe from
addition, defect or alteration. Its copies should be
spread in every place and written with a living

language that is read by millions of people, who can convey the Messege of Allâh to all mankind. This Book is the Magnificent Qur'ân which Allâh revealed to Muhammad ﷺ and that is the witness over all the previous Books and it confirms them - before they were interpolated. It is the Book that all mankind must follow, so that, it can be for them, light, healing, guidance and mercy. Allâh says,

﴿وَهَذَا كِتَبٌ أَنزَلْنَهُ مُبَارَكٌ فَٱتَّبِعُوهُ وَٱتَّقُواْ لَعَلَّكُمْ تُرْحَمُونَ﴾

"And this is a Blessed Book which We have sent down, so follow it and fear Allâh that you may receive mercy."[1]

He also says,

﴿قُلْ يَأَيُّهَا ٱلنَّاسُ إِنِّى رَسُولُ ٱللَّهِ إِلَيْكُمْ جَمِيعًا﴾

"Say (O Muhammad): O mankind! Verily, I am sent to you all as the Messenger of Allâh."[2]

Four: Belief in the Messengers

To believe that Allâh sent Messengers to His creation in order to give them glad tidings of Paradise if they believe in Allâh and believe in the Messengers, and to warn them of punishment if they disobey. Allâh says,

﴿وَلَقَدْ بَعَثْنَا فِى كُلِّ أُمَّةٍ رَّسُولًا أَنِ ٱعْبُدُواْ ٱللَّهَ وَٱجْتَنِبُواْ ٱلطَّغُوتَ﴾

---

[1] Al-An'âm 6:155.

[2] Al-A'râf 7:158. For all the above, see: Al-Aqeedatu-s-saheehah p. 17; Aqeedatu ahlis-sunnah waljamaa'ah p. 22; Mabaadiul Islâm p. 89.

"And verily, We have sent among every nation a Messenger (proclaiming): Worship Allâh (alone) and avoid all false deities."[1]

He also says,

﴿رُّسُلًا مُّبَشِّرِينَ وَمُنذِرِينَ لِئَلَّا يَكُونَ لِلنَّاسِ عَلَى ٱللَّهِ حُجَّةٌ بَعْدَ ٱلرُّسُلِ﴾

"Messengers as bearers of good news as well as of warning in order that mankind should have no plea against Allâh after the (coming of) Messengers."[2]

These Messengers are many. The first of them was Noah and the last of them is Muhammad. There are many among them, those whom Allâh told us stories about like Abraham, Moses, Jesus, David, John Zakariah and Sâlih. There are also some about whom Allâh tells us nothing. Allâh says,

﴿وَرُسُلًا قَدْ فَصَصْنَـٰهُمْ عَلَيْكَ مِن قَبْلُ وَرُسُلًا لَّمْ نَقْصُصْهُمْ عَلَيْكَ﴾

"And Messengers We have mentioned to you before and Messengers We have not mentioned to you."[3]

All these Messengers were humans created by Allâh. They possessed nothing of the qualities of Lordship or Godship. Therefore, no act of worship should be directed to them; for they could avail themselves of any harm or benefit. Allâh says about Prophet Noah,

---

[1] An-Nahl 16:36.

[2] An-Nisâ' 4:165.

[3] An-Nisâ' 4:164.

﴿وَلَا أَقُولُ لَكُمْ عِندِى خَزَآئِنُ ٱللَّهِ وَلَا أَعْلَمُ ٱلْغَيْبَ وَلَا أَقُولُ إِنِّى مَلَكٌ﴾

"And I do not say to you that with me are the Treasures of Allâh, nor that I know the Unseen, nor do I say I am an angel."[1]

Allâh also Commanded Muhammad to say,

﴿قُل لَّا أَقُولُ لَكُمْ عِندِى خَزَآئِنُ ٱللَّهِ وَلَا أَعْلَمُ ٱلْغَيْبَ وَلَا أَقُولُ لَكُمْ إِنِّى مَلَكٌ﴾

"I do not tell you that with me are the Treasures of Allâh, nor that I know the Unseen, nor do I tell you that I am an angel."[2]

And to say,

﴿قُل لَّا أَمْلِكُ لِنَفْسِى نَفْعًا وَلَا ضَرًّا إِلَّا مَا شَآءَ ٱللَّهُ﴾

"I possess no power over benefit or hurt to myself except as Allâh Wills."[3]

The Prophets are therefore honoured slaves, whom Allâh chose and honoured with the Message and described as His slaves. Their religion is Islâm and Allâh will not accept any other religion besides it. Allâh says,

﴿إِنَّ ٱلدِّينَ عِندَ ٱللَّهِ ٱلْإِسْلَٰمُ﴾

"Verily, the religion with Allâh is Islâm."[4]

---

[1] Hood 11:31.
[2] Al-An'âm 6:50.
[3] Al-A'râf 7:188.
[4] Aal Imrân 3:19.

The basic messages of the Prophets were one but their Laws differ. Allâh says,

$$﴿لِكُلٍّ جَعَلْنَا مِنكُمْ شِرْعَةً وَمِنْهَاجًا﴾$$

"To each among you We have prescribed a Law and a Clear Way."[1]

The final of all these Laws is that of Muhammad ﷺ. It abrogates all other previous laws. His Message is the last of all Divine Messages and he is the last of all Messengers. Whoever believes in a Prophet among them should believe in all of them and whoever denies anyone of them has denied all of them; for all Prophets and Messengers call to the belief in Allâh, His angels, His Books, His Messengers and the Last Day and because their religion is one. So, he who disbelieves in others has disbelieved in all of them; for every one of them called to belief in all Prophets and Messengers.[2] Allâh says,

$$﴿ءَامَنَ ٱلرَّسُولُ بِمَآ أُنزِلَ إِلَيْهِ مِن رَّبِّهِۦ وَٱلْمُؤْمِنُونَ ۚ كُلٌّ ءَامَنَ بِٱللَّهِ وَمَلَٰٓئِكَتِهِۦ وَكُتُبِهِۦ وَرُسُلِهِۦ﴾$$

"The Messenger believes in what has been sent down to him from his Lord and so do the believers. Each one believes in Allâh, His angels, His Books and His Messengers"[3]

He also says,

---

[1] Al-Mâ'idah 5:48.

[2] See: *Al-Aqeedatus-saheehah* p. 17; *Aqeedatu ah lus-sunnah waljamaa'ah* p. 25.

[3] Al-Baqarah 2:285.

﴿إِنَّ ٱلَّذِينَ يَكْفُرُونَ بِٱللَّهِ وَرُسُلِهِ وَيُرِيدُونَ أَن يُفَرِّقُوا۟ بَيْنَ ٱللَّهِ وَرُسُلِهِ وَيَقُولُونَ نُؤْمِنُ بِبَعْضٍ وَنَكْفُرُ بِبَعْضٍ وَيُرِيدُونَ أَن يَتَّخِذُوا۟ بَيْنَ ذَٰلِكَ سَبِيلًا ۝ أُو۟لَٰٓئِكَ هُمُ ٱلْكَٰفِرُونَ حَقًّا وَأَعْتَدْنَا لِلْكَٰفِرِينَ عَذَابًا مُّهِينًا ۝﴾

"Verily, those who disbelieve in Allâh and His Messengers and wish to make distinction between Allâh and His Messengers saying: We believe in some (Messengers) but reject others, and wish to adopt a way in between. They are in truth, disbelievers. And We have prepared for the disbelievers a humiliating torment."[1]

Five: Belief in the Last Day

That is because, the end of every being in this world is death! What then is the fate of man after death? What is the end of the unjust people who escaped the punishment in this world?, Will they escape the consequence of their injustices? What about the righteous people who missed their share of the reward of this world, are their rewards going to be wasted?

Indeed, mankind shall continue to die, generation after generation, until when Allâh gives His permission that this world should come to an end and all creatures on the face of the earth die. Allâh will thereafter resurrect all creatures in a day that will be witnessed by all; a day in which Allâh will gather all former and later generations. He will then call men to account for all

---

[1] An-Nisâ' 4:150-151.

their deeds either good or bad which they had earned in the world. The believers will be led to Paradise and the disbelievers will be marched to Fire.

Paradise is the abode of peace which He has prepared for His believing friends. There are in it all kinds of bliss which no one can describe. It has degrees and every degree will have dwellers according to the degree of their belief in Allâh and their obedience to Him. The lowest in degree of the dwellers of Paradise in bliss will be equal to tenfold of the Kingdom of one of the kings of this world.

Hell is the abode of punishment which Allâh has prepared for him who disbelieves in Him. It has all kinds of torment whose mere mention is terrifying. If Allâh will allow anyone to die in the Hereafter the dwellers of the Fire will certainly die at mere sight of it.

Allâh knows - by His Pre-Knowledge - what every man will do or say of good or evil, secretly or publicly. He assigned to every man two angels: one records his good deeds and the other his evil ones and nothing escapes them. Allâh says,

$$\text{﴿مَّا يَلْفِظُ مِن قَوْلٍ إِلَّا لَدَيْهِ رَقِيبٌ عَتِيدٌ﴾}$$

"Not a word does he utter but there is a watcher by him ready (to record it)."[1]

All his deeds will be recorded in a book that will be given to man on the Day of Resurrection. Allâh says,

$$\text{﴿وَوُضِعَ ٱلْكِتَٰبُ فَتَرَى ٱلْمُجْرِمِينَ مُشْفِقِينَ مِمَّا فِيهِ وَيَقُولُونَ يَٰوَيْلَتَنَا}$$

---

[1] Qaaf 50:18.

مَالِ هَذَا ٱلْكِتَبِ لَا يُغَادِرُ صَغِيرَةً وَلَا كَبِيرَةً إِلَّا أَحْصَنهَا وَوَجَدُواْ
مَا عَمِلُواْ حَاضِرًا وَلَا يَظْلِمُ رَبُّكَ أَحَدًا﴾

"And the book (one's record) will be placed, and you
will see the sinners fearful of that which is (recorded)
therein. They will say: 'Woe to us! What sort of book
is this that leaves neither a small thing nor a big thing,
but has recorded it with numbers.' And they will find
all that they did, placed before them, and your Lord
treats no one with injustice." [1]

The man will then read his record and will not deny
anything therein and whosoever denies anything of
his deeds, Allâh will give power of speech to his ears,
eyes, hands, legs and skin, so that they could
contradict him. Allâh says,

﴿وَقَالُواْ لِجُلُودِهِمْ لِمَ شَهِدتُّمْ عَلَيْنَا قَالُواْ أَنطَقَنَا ٱللَّهُ ٱلَّذِىٓ أَنطَقَ كُلَّ
شَىْءٍ وَهُوَ خَلَقَكُمْ أَوَّلَ مَرَّةٍ وَإِلَيْهِ تُرْجَعُونَ ○وَمَا كُنتُمْ تَسْتَتِرُونَ أَن
يَشْهَدَ عَلَيْكُمْ سَمْعُكُمْ وَلَا أَبْصَرُكُمْ وَلَا جُلُودُكُمْ وَلَكِن ظَنَنتُمْ أَنَّ ٱللَّهَ
لَا يَعْلَمُ كَثِيرًا مِّمَّا تَعْمَلُونَ﴾

"And they will say to their skins: 'Why do you testify
against us?' They will say: 'Allâh has caused us to
speak - and He causes all things to speak: and He
created you the first time and to Him you are made to
return. And you have not been hiding yourselves (in
the world) lest your ears, your eyes and your skins
should testify against you; but you thought that Allâh
knew not much of what you were doing." [2]

---

[1] Al-Kahf 18:49.
[2] Fussilat 41:21-22.

Belief in the Last Day[1] - Day of Resurrection - was preached by all Messengers and Prophets. Allâh says,

﴿وَمِنْ ءَايَـٰتِهِۦٓ أَنَّكَ تَرَى ٱلْأَرْضَ خَـٰشِعَةً فَإِذَآ أَنزَلْنَا عَلَيْهَا ٱلْمَآءَ ٱهْتَزَّتْ وَرَبَتْ إِنَّ ٱلَّذِىٓ أَحْيَاهَا لَمُحْىِ ٱلْمَوْتَىٰٓ إِنَّهُۥ عَلَىٰ كُلِّ شَىْءٍ قَدِيرٌ﴾

"And among His signs is that you see the earth barren; but when We send down water (rain) to it, it is stirred to life and growth (of vegetations). Verily, He Who gives it life, surely, is Able to give life to the dead (on the Day of Resurrection). Indeed, He is Able to do all things."[2]

He also says,

﴿أَوَلَمْ يَرَوْا۟ أَنَّ ٱللَّهَ ٱلَّذِى خَلَقَ ٱلسَّمَـٰوَٰتِ وَٱلْأَرْضَ وَلَمْ يَعْىَ بِخَلْقِهِنَّ بِقَـٰدِرٍ عَلَىٰٓ أَن يُحْـۧىَ ٱلْمَوْتَىٰ﴾

"Do they not see that Allâh, Who created the heavens and the earth, and was not wearied by their creation, is Able to give life to the dead?"[3]

This is what the Divine Wisdom necessitates; for Allâh did not create His creation in vain or leave them for fun. The weakest person in intelligence cannot carry out any important action without having a purpose for it. How can this not be imagined in case of man and then think that Allâh only created His creation for fun and that He shall leave them in vain. Far and Highly Exalted is Allâh above all that they say. Allâh says,

---

[1] For more evidences about resurrection, see pages 82-90 of this book.

[2] Fussilat 41:39.

[3] Al-Ahqâf 46:33.

﴿أَفَحَسِبْتُمْ أَنَّمَا خَلَقْنَاكُمْ عَبَثًا وَأَنَّكُمْ إِلَيْنَا لَا تُرْجَعُونَ﴾

"Do you think that We had created you in play (without any purpose) and that you would not be brought back to Us?"[1]

He also says,

﴿وَمَا خَلَقْنَا ٱلسَّمَآءَ وَٱلْأَرْضَ وَمَا بَيْنَهُمَا بَٰطِلًا ذَٰلِكَ ظَنُّ ٱلَّذِينَ كَفَرُوا۟ فَوَيْلٌ لِّلَّذِينَ كَفَرُوا۟ مِنَ ٱلنَّارِ﴾

"And We created not the heaven and the earth and all that is between them without purpose! That is the assumption of those who disbelieve! Then woe to those who disbelieve (in Islâmic Monotheism) from the Fire."[2]

All wise men testify to the necessity of belief in the Last Day; for that's what the intelligence and reason necessitate and what the sound human nature agrees to. When man believes in the Day of Resurrection, he knows why he should abstain from what he is ordered to leave and do what he is ordered to do, hoping for what is with Allâh. He will also know that, he who does injustice to people will inevitably have his recompense and that those he wrongs will take revenge on him on the Day of Resurrection. He will also know that man must have a reward: good reward for good deeds and commensurate punishment for evil deeds, so that each soul shall be rewarded for what it strived for and Divine Justice can be established. Allâh says,

---

[1] Al-Mu'minûn 23:115.

[2] Sâd 38:27.

$$﴿فَمَن يَعْمَلْ مِثْقَالَ ذَرَّةٍ خَيْرًا يَرَهُ ۝ وَمَن يَعْمَلْ مِثْقَالَ ذَرَّةٍ شَرًّا يَرَهُ ۝﴾$$

"So whoever does an atom weight of good shall see it; and whoever does an atom weight of evil shall see it." [1]

No one among mankind knows when the Day of Resurrection will come. This is a Day that is known to neither a sent Prophet nor a favoured Angel. Allâh keeps the knowledge of that to Himself alone. He says,

$$﴿يَسْأَلُونَكَ عَنِ ٱلسَّاعَةِ أَيَّانَ مُرْسَىٰهَا قُلْ إِنَّمَا عِلْمُهَا عِندَ رَبِّي لَا يُجَلِّيهَا لِوَقْتِهَا إِلَّا هُوَ﴾$$

"They ask you about the Hour (Day of Resurrection): 'When will be its appointed time?' Say: 'The Knowledge thereof is with my Lord. None can reveal its time but He.' " [2]

He also says,

$$﴿إِنَّ ٱللَّهَ عِندَهُ عِلْمُ ٱلسَّاعَةِ﴾$$

"Verily, with Allâh is the knowledge of the Hour." [3]

Six: Belief in Pre-decree

You must believe that Allâh knows what happens and what shall happen; that He knows the conditions, deeds, life spans and provisions of His slaves. He says,

$$﴿إِنَّ ٱللَّهَ بِكُلِّ شَيْءٍ عَلِيمٌ﴾$$

---

[1] Zalzalah 99:7-8.
[2] Al-A'râf 7:187.
[3] Luqmân 31:34.

"Verily, Allâh is All-Knower of everything." [1]

He also says,

﴿وَعِندَهُۥ مَفَاتِحُ ٱلْغَيْبِ لَا يَعْلَمُهَآ إِلَّا هُوَ وَيَعْلَمُ مَا فِي ٱلْبَرِّ وَٱلْبَحْرِ وَمَا تَسْقُطُ مِن وَرَقَةٍ إِلَّا يَعْلَمُهَا وَلَا حَبَّةٍ فِي ظُلُمَٰتِ ٱلْأَرْضِ وَلَا رَطْبٍ وَلَا يَابِسٍ إِلَّا فِي كِتَٰبٍ مُّبِينٍ﴾

"And with Him are the keys of all that is hidden, none knows them but He. And He knows whatever there is in the land and in the sea; not a leaf falls but He knows it. There is not a grain in the darkness of the earth nor anything fresh or dry, but is written in a Clear Record." [2]

He registers all that in a Record with Him. He also says,

﴿وَكُلَّ شَىْءٍ أَحْصَيْنَٰهُ فِىٓ إِمَامٍ مُّبِينٍ﴾

"And all things We have recorded with numbers (as a record) in a Clear Book." [3]

---

[1] Al-'Ankabût 29:62.

[2] Al-An'âm 6:59. Had not there been in the Qur'ân but only this verse, it would have been enough as a clear evidence and decisive proof that it is from Allâh; for mankind, in all their ages — even in this age, where knowledge is widespread and man grows arrogant — have not thought of this comprehensive encompassment, let alone having the ability to do any of that. The highest extent to which their efforts could carry them is to closely observe a tree or insect in a particular environment, in order to reveal to us a part of its mysteries. But what is hidden from them in that tree or insect is greater. As for comprehensive think and encompassment, it is a matter that mankind have not known or have the ability to know.

[3] Yâ-Sîn 36:12.

He says,

$$﴿أَلَمْ تَعْلَمْ أَنَّ اللَّهَ يَعْلَمُ مَا فِي السَّمَاءِ وَالْأَرْضِ إِنَّ ذَلِكَ فِي كِتَابٍ إِنَّ ذَلِكَ عَلَى اللَّهِ يَسِيرٌ﴾$$

"Know you not that Allâh knows all that is in the heavens and on the earth? Verily, it is (all) in the Book. Verily, that is easy for Allâh."[1]

He also says,

$$﴿إِنَّمَا أَمْرُهُ إِذَا أَرَادَ شَيْئًا أَن يَقُولَ لَهُ كُن فَيَكُونُ﴾$$

"Verily, His Command, when He intends a thing, is only that He says to it, 'Be' and it is!"[2]

As it is Allâh Who preordained all things, it is also He Who Created all things. He says,

$$﴿إِنَّا كُلَّ شَيْءٍ خَلَقْنَاهُ بِقَدَرٍ﴾$$

"Verily, We have created everything with Divine Preordainment."[3]

He also says,

$$﴿اللَّهُ خَالِقُ كُلِّ شَيْءٍ﴾$$

"Allâh is the Creator of all things."[4]

He created men in order to worship Him and made that clear to them. He commanded them to obey Him, forbidden them from disobeying Him and made that

---

[1] Al-Hajj 22:70.
[2] Yâ-Sîn 36:82.
[3] Al-Qamar 54:49.
[4] Az-Zumar 39:62.

clear to them. He gave them power and will by which they could carry out the Commandments of Allâh and get reward; and by which they could perpetrate acts of disobedience, and get punished.

If man believes in the Divine Pre-ordainment, he will achieve the following:

1. He will depend on Allâh while making use of the means; for he knows that the means and its causes are all by Divine Pre-decree of Allâh.

2. Peace of mind and tranquillity; for when he knows that it is Allâh Who gives that and that the preordained detestable thing shall happen no matter what, he will have rest of mind and he will be pleased with the decision of Allâh. There will not be anyone who will be more pleased and have more peace of mind than him Who believes in Divine Preordainment.

3. He will not be arrogant when he attains what he aims; for he will know that the attainment of that blessing is from Allâh through the means of good and success He has pre-decreed. He will therefore thank Allâh for that.

4. He will not be sad or distressed when the desired goal is missed or when the unwanted happens; because of his knowledge that it happens through irresistible Decree of Allâh. For no one can resist His Command or appeal His judgement. What he has pre-decreed will inevitably happen. He will therefore be patient and get the reward thereof from Allâh. Allâh says,

$$\text{﴿مَا أَصَابَ مِن مُّصِيبَةٍ فِي ٱلْأَرْضِ وَلَا فِي أَنفُسِكُمْ إِلَّا فِي كِتَابٍ}$$

$$\text{مِّن قَبْلِ أَن نَّبْرَأَهَا إِنَّ ذَٰلِكَ عَلَى ٱللَّهِ يَسِيرٌ ○ لِّكَيْلَا تَأْسَوْا عَلَى مَا}$$

$$\text{فَاتَكُمْ وَلَا تَفْرَحُوا بِمَا ءَاتَىٰكُمْ وَٱللَّهُ لَا يُحِبُّ كُلَّ مُخْتَالٍ فَخُورٍ﴾}$$

"No calamity befalls on earth or in yourselves, but it is inscribed in the Book of Decrees before We bring it into existence. Verily, that is easy for Allâh. In order that you may not grieve at the things that you fail to get, nor rejoice over that which has been given to you. And Allâh likes not prideful boasters."[1]

5. Complete dependence on Allâh. For the Muslim knows that, it is only Allâh Who has the power to cause benefit or harm. He will then not fear any powerful person because of his power and will not hesitate to do good deeds out of fear of any man. The Prophet ﷺ told Ibn Abbas:

$$\text{«وَاعْلَمْ أَنَّ الْأُمَّةَ لَوِ اجْتَمَعَتْ عَلَى أَنْ يَنْفَعُوكَ بِشَيْءٍ لَمْ}$$

$$\text{يَنْفَعُوكَ إِلَّا بِشَيْءٍ قَدْ كَتَبَهُ اللهُ لَكَ، وَإِنِ اجْتَمَعُوا عَلَى أَنْ}$$

$$\text{يَضُرُّوكَ بِشَيْءٍ لَمْ يَضُرُّوكَ إِلَّا بِشَيْءٍ قَدْ كَتَبَهُ الله عَلَيْكَ»}$$

"Know that if all mankind are unanimous on benefiting you, they cannot benefit you with anything except with that which Allâh has predecreed for you. If they are also unanimous on harming you, they cannot harm you except with that which Allâh has predecreed for you."[2]

---

[1] Al-Hadeed 57:22-23. See: *Al-Aqeedah as-saheehah* p. 19; *Aqeedah ahlisunnah wal jamaa'ah* p. 39 and *Deenul Haqq* p. 18.

[2] Ahmad and At-Tirmidhee.

The Third Degree

The third degree is "*Ihsaan*" (utmost sincerity and perfection in acts of worship). It implies which means that you worship Allâh as if you are seeing Him, and if you do not see Him, He sees you. One must worship his Lord with this quality. That is, to bear it in mind that Allâh is close to him; that he is standing before his Lord. This condition makes man have awe, fear and great honour for Allâh. It makes man sincere in acts of worship and gives him courage to strive more towards its perfection.

The slave is conscious of his Lord while observing act of worship and reminds himself of His nearness to him as if he is seeing Him. If he cannot do that, let him be conscious of the fact that Allâh sees him and knows his secret and public affairs, and that nothing is hidden from Him.[1]

The slave that has reached this stage worships his Lord sincerely, not looking to others besides Him. He neither expects people's praise nor fears their blame; for it is enough for him that his Lord is pleased with him and praises him. This is a man whose public and private deeds are the same. He worships his Lord in private and public with certain faith that Allâh knows all that is in his heart and goes on in his mind. The faith has overpowered his heart and the consciousness of his Lord is manifest on him; his limbs then surrender to Allâh; for he will not use them except

---

[1] *Jaamiul 'uloom wal-Hikam* p. 128.

in what pleases Allâh and in that which He loves and in submission to Him.

Since his heart has been attached to his Lord, he will not seek help from any creature, for Allâh suffices him; he will not complain to any man, for he has approached Allâh with his needs and enough is He as a Helper. He does not feel lonely in any place nor does he fear anyone, for he knows that Allâh is with him in all his conditions. He is enough for him and He is the Best Helper. He will not abandon any order that Allâh commands him to carry out and will not perpetrate any sin, for he is ashamed before Him and hates that He finds him wanting in what He Commands him to do or finds him where He forbids him. He will neither oppress nor wrong anyone or take anyone's right for he knows that Allâh is seeing him, and that He shall call him to account for all his deeds.

He will not cause mischief in the land; for he knows that all good things that are in the earth are properties of Allâh which He subjects for His Creation. He will take of these good things according to his needs and thank his Lord for facilitating them for him.

All that I have told you and presented to you in this booklet are only important matters and great pillars in Islâm. Whoever believes in these fundamentals and acts by them has become a Muslim. If not, Islâm - as I have told you - is both a religion and a way of life. It is the comprehensive and perfect Divine Order that encompasses in its ordainments all that the individual and the society need in all aspects of their religious, political, economical, social and security life. Man will find therein principles, fundamentals and rules that regulate peace and war and binding duties; and preserves the dignity of man, bird, animals and the environment that surrounds him. They also explain to him the reality of man, the life and the death; and the Resurrection after death. He also finds in Islâm the best methodology of relating with people around him; such as the saying of Allâh,

$$﴿وَقُولُواْ لِلنَّاسِ حُسْنًا﴾$$

"And speak good to people"[1]

And His saying,

$$﴿وَٱلْعَافِينَ عَنِ ٱلنَّاسِ﴾$$

"And those who pardon men."[2]

And His saying,

$$﴿وَلَا يَجْرِمَنَّكُمْ شَنَآنُ قَوْمٍ عَلَىٰٓ أَلَّا تَعْدِلُواْ ٱعْدِلُواْ هُوَ أَقْرَبُ لِلتَّقْوَىٰ﴾$$

"And let not the enmity and hatred of others make you avoid justice. Be just; that is nearer to piety."[3]

After we have discussed the degrees of this religion and the fundamentals of each degree, it is appropriate that we discuss briefly the beauties of Islâm.

---

[1] Al-Baqarah 2:83.
[2] Aal Imrân 3:134.
[3] Al-Mâ'idah 5:8.

Some Beauties of Islâm[1]

The beauties of Islâm are beyond what pens can fully write and enough expressions cannot be found to describe the virtues of this religion; because it is the religion of Allâh. Just as the eye cannot encompass the perception of Allâh and man cannot encompass His Reality on Knowledge, so can the pen not encompass His Law in description. Ibn Al-Qayyim said, "If you reflect on the dazzling wisdom in this Upright Religion, this pure faith and the Law enacted for mankind, which no expression can perfectly describe, whose description cannot be perfected, the likeness of which the wisdom of the wise cannot propose - even if all wise men are to be as perfectly wise as the wisest one among them, whose beauty and virtues are perceived and attested to by the perfect and honourable intelligence, that the world had not known a law better and greater than it even if the Messenger of Allâh ﷺ had not brought any proof in support of it, all that would have been enough an evidence that it is from Allâh. Every aspect of this religion shows perfect knowledge, perfect wisdom, expansiveness of mercy, righteousness and kindness, absolute inclusion of all that is hidden and manifest and the knowledge about the beginnings and ends. It also shows that it is one of the greatest favours that Allâh has bestowed on His slaves, for He bestows not

---

[1] For more detail on this section, read *Ad-Durratul mukhtasarah fee mahaasiniddeenil Islâmee*, by Shaykh Abdur-Rahmaan As-Sa'dee; and *Mahaasinul Islâm*, by Shaykh Abdul Azeez As-Salmaan.

on them a favour greater than the fact that He guided them to this religion, made them its adherents and chosen it for them. Hence, He reminds His slaves of the fact that He guided them to it. He says,

﴿لَقَدْ مَنَّ ٱللَّهُ عَلَى ٱلْمُؤْمِنِينَ إِذْ بَعَثَ فِيهِمْ رَسُولًا مِّنْ أَنفُسِهِمْ يَتْلُواْ عَلَيْهِمْ ءَايَٰتِهِۦ وَيُزَكِّيهِمْ وَيُعَلِّمُهُمُ ٱلْكِتَٰبَ وَٱلْحِكْمَةَ وَإِن كَانُواْ مِن قَبْلُ لَفِى ضَلَٰلٍ مُّبِينٍ﴾

"Indeed, Allâh conferred a great favour on the believers when He sent among them a Messenger (Muhammad ﷺ) from among themselves reciting unto them His Verses (the Qur'ân), purifying them and instructing them in the Book and the wisdom (the Sunnah) while before that they had been in manifest error."[1]

He also says, making Himself known to His slaves and reminding them of His great favour on them, calling them to thank Him for making them among its adherents,

﴿ٱلْيَوْمَ أَكْمَلْتُ لَكُمْ دِينَكُمْ﴾

"This day, I have perfected your religion for you."[2]

It is therefore part of showing gratitude to Allâh on this religion, to mention some of its beauties:

1. That it is the religion of Allâh which He has chosen for Himself, sent with His Messengers and by which He allowed His slaves to worship Him. His

---

[1] Aal Imrân 3:164.
[2] Al-Mâ'idah 5:3, See: Miftaahu daaris Sa'aadah V. 1, p. 374-375.

religion is not comparable to human statutes and man-made religions. As Allâh possesses the quality of absolute perfection, so does His religion has an absolute perfection in providing ordainments that reform the worldly and eternal life of mankind; encompasses the rights of the Creator and obligations of His slaves towards Him; obligations of one towards another and the rights of each one of them upon another.

2. Comprehensiveness: One of the most prominent beauties of this religion is its comprehensiveness for everything. Allâh says,

$$﴿مَّا فَرَّطْنَا فِى ٱلْكِتَبِ مِن شَىْءٍ﴾$$

"We have neglected nothing in the Book."[1]

This religion encompasses all that has to do with the Creator like His Names, Attributes and rights; and all that has to do with the creatures like laws, obligations, manners and relationship. This religion also encompasses the stories of former and latter generations, stories of angels, Prophets and Messengers. It tells about the heaven, the earth, the orbits, the planets, seas, trees and the universe. It mentions the goal and aim of creation and its end; talks about Paradise and the final abode of the believers and Fire and the final abode of disbelievers.

3. It establishes a connection between the Creator and the creation: Every false religion 4and creed has the

---

[1] Al-An'âm 6:38.

character of linking man with another man that is prone to death, weakness, incapacity and diseases. Some even link man to a person who has died since hundreds of years ago and had become mere bones and dust. Islâm, on the other hand, has the quality of linking man to his Creator directly; with no priest nor reverend and no holy secret. If this direct connection between the Creator and the created; a connection that links the heart with its Lord and it thereby gets light, guidance and loftiness; seeks for perfection; and deems itself high above insignificant and debased things. For every heart that has no link with its Lord is more erroneous than animals.

It is a communication between the Creator and the creature by which he knows the wish of his Creator and then worship Him with the knowledge, and gets to know things that please Him and seek for that, and things that annoys Him and shun them. It is a communication between the All-Mighty Creator and the weak and destitute creature, that enables him seek for aid, assistance and success from Him, and ask Him for protection against evil planners and evil deeds of devils.

4. It caters for benefits of this world and the Hereafter. The Islâmic Law is based on protection of the benefits of this world and the Hereafter and on perfection of good morals. As for the explanation of the benefits of the Hereafter, the religion of Islâm has explained all that and left nothing of it not taken care of. It explains it in detail so that nothing of it may be unknown. Islâm promises the bliss in

the Hereafter and warns against its torment.

Concerning the benefits of this world, Allâh ordained in this religion what can protect for man his religion, life, property, posterity, dignity and intelligence.

Concerning honourable conducts, Islâm enjoins that overtly and covertly and forbids debasing manners. Among the apparent noble conducts that Islâm enjoins are cleanliness and purification from all kinds of impurities and dirt. Islâm recommends using of perfume and outward adornment; it forbids filthy behaviours like adultery and fornication, consuming alcohol; eating dead animals, blood and pork flesh, and enjoins eating of lawful good things. It also prohibits wastefulness and extravagance.

As for inner purification, Islâm prohibits undesirable conducts and encourages commendable ones. Among the forbidden manners are: lies, obscenity, anger, jealousy, stinginess, debasing oneself, love of prestige and this world, arrogance, haughtiness and hypocrisy. Among the commended behaviours are: good conduct, good companionship to all people and being kind to them, justice and fairness, humility, truthfulness, magnanimity, generosity, dependence on Allâh, sincerity in acts of worship, fear of Allâh, patience and showing gratitude.[1]

5. Easiness: Easiness is one of the unique qualities of

---

[1] See: Al-'I'laam bimaa fee deenin-nasaaraa minal fasaad wal-awhaam, by Al-Qurtubee p. 442-445.

this religion. In every ritual is easiness and in every act of worship is easiness. Allâh says,

$$﴿وَمَا جَعَلَ عَلَيْكُمْ فِي ٱلدِّينِ مِنْ حَرَجٍ﴾$$

"He has not laid upon you in religion any hardship"[1]

The first easiness in Islâm is that; anyone who wants to become a Muslim does not need a human intermediary or a confession of past sins. He only needs to cleanse himself and utter the statement: I testify that there is no deity worthy of worship except Allâh and I testify that Muhammad is the Messenger of Allâh; and to believe in the meanings of this statement and act by its implications.

Further, every worship in Islâm is characterised by easiness and alleviation. If a man travels or is sick, the reward of the deed that he used to do when he was at home or healthy will continue to be recorded to his credit. The whole life of the Muslim is easy and filled with tranquillity, while the life of a disbeliever is conversely filled with hardship and toil. Also, the death of a Muslim is easy where his soul comes out of his body as a drop of water comes out of a vessel. Allâh says,

$$﴿ٱلَّذِينَ تَتَوَفَّىٰهُمُ ٱلْمَلَٰئِكَةُ طَيِّبِينَ يَقُولُونَ سَلَٰمٌ عَلَيْكُمُ ٱدْخُلُوا۟ ٱلْجَنَّةَ بِمَا كُنتُمْ تَعْمَلُونَ﴾$$

"Those whose lives the angels take while they are pious saying (to them): peace be on you, enter

---
[1] Al-Hajj 22:78

Paradise because of that (the good) which you used to do (in the world)." [1]

As for the disbeliever, the stern and harsh angels will be present at his death beating him with lashes. Allâh says about the disbeliever,

﴿وَلَوْ تَرَىٰٓ إِذِ ٱلظَّٰلِمُونَ فِى غَمَرَٰتِ ٱلْمَوْتِ وَٱلْمَلَٰٓئِكَةُ بَاسِطُوٓاْ أَيْدِيهِمْ أَخْرِجُوٓاْ أَنفُسَكُمُ ٱلْيَوْمَ تُجْزَوْنَ عَذَابَ ٱلْهُونِ بِمَا كُنتُمْ تَقُولُونَ عَلَى ٱللَّهِ غَيْرَ ٱلْحَقِّ وَكُنتُمْ عَنْ ءَايَٰتِهِۦ تَسْتَكْبِرُونَ﴾

"And if you could but see when the wrong-doers are in the agonies of death, while the angels are stretching forth their hands (saying): Deliver your soul, this day, you shall be recompensed with the torment of degradation because of what you used to utter against Allâh other than the truth. And you used to reject His revelations with disrespect." [2]

He also says,

﴿وَلَوْ تَرَىٰٓ إِذْ يَتَوَفَّى ٱلَّذِينَ كَفَرُوٓاْ ٱلْمَلَٰٓئِكَةُ يَضْرِبُونَ وُجُوهَهُمْ وَأَدْبَٰرَهُمْ وَذُوقُواْ عَذَابَ ٱلْحَرِيقِ﴾

"And if you could see when the angels take away the souls of those who disbelieve (at death); they smite their faces and their backs (saying): Taste the punishment of the blazing Fire." [3]

6. Justice: The one who ordains the Islâmic injunctions is Allâh alone. He is the Creator of all people: black and white, male and female. Men are equal before

---

[1] An-Nahl 16:32.
[2] Al-An'âm 6:93.
[3] Al-Anfâl 8:50.

His judgement, justice and mercy. He ordains rules
that suits each of the male and female. It then
becomes impossible that the Law of Islâm favours
male at the expense of female or gives female
preference and do injustice to male. Islâm also does
not endow white man with qualities and deny that
to the black man. All are equal before the Laws of
Allâh and no difference between them except by
piety.

7. Enjoining all that is good and forbidding all that is
evil: The religion of Islâm has noble characteristics,
which is enjoining all that is good and forbidding
all that is evil. This duty is incumbent on every
male or female Muslim who is an adult, sane and
able to enjoin and forbid according to his or her
ability and according to the degrees of the enjoining
and prohibition. He or she should command or
forbid with hand, if not able to do so then with the
tongue and if not able then with the heart. By this
all members of the Muslim community will be
supervisors in the community.

Every individual should command whoever is
negligent to do good deed, and forbid whoever does
wrong to desist, be he either a ruler or ruled; each
according to his ability and in accordance with Islâmic
regulations that control this matter.

This matter - as you can see - is compulsory upon
individual according to his ability. Compare this to
what the contemporary political orders proudly claim
that they give opportunity to opposition parties to
monitor the government activities and carry out

official functions.

These are some of the beauties of Islâm. Had I wanted to go into details, I would have stopped at every rite, every obligation, every commandment and every prohibition in order to explain the extensive wisdom, decisive ordainment, impressive, unique and matchless perfection that lie therein. Whoever ponders over the ordainments of this religion, he will know with certainty that it is from Allâh and that it is the truth that is free of any doubt and a guidance from error. If you therefore want to go back to Allâh, to follow His Law and to follow the path of His Prophets and Messengers, the door of repentance is open before you and your Lord is Oft-Forgiving, Most -Merciful. He calls you in order to forgive you.

Repentance

The Messenger of Allâh ﷺ said,

«كُلُّ ابْنِ آدَمَ خَطَّاءٌ، وَخَيْرُ الْخَطَّائِينَ التَّوَّابُونَ»

"All children of Adam do commit sins and the best of the sinners are those who repent."[1]

Man by nature is weak; he is weak in his aim and resolution and is unable to bear the consequences of his sins and misdeeds. So Allâh, out of kindness, makes matters easy for man and He prescribed for him repentance.

The essence of repentance is to abandon the sin because of its ugliness - out of fear for Allâh- and out of desire for His Mercy; to regret over what one has done, to determine not to go back to the sin again and to spend whatever is left of one's life in good deeds.[2]

As you can see, repentance is a deed of the heart that is pure between the slave and his Lord. It is neither a hard nor difficult job for him; it is just a deed of the heart, to abandon the sin, and not to go back to it. There are, in abstention from all that Allâh forbid, well-being and peace of mind.[3]

You do not need to repent at the hand of a man who will reveal your secret and manipulate your weakness. It is only a communication between you and your Lord; you seek His forgiveness and guidance and He

---

[1] Tirmidhi (2499), Ibn Majah (4251), Ahmad (13049).

[2] *Al-Mufradaat fee ghareebil Qur'ân*, p. 76, quoted freely.

[3] *Al-Fawaaid* by Ibn Al-Qayyim.

forgives you. There is nothing like inherited sin in Islâm, nor is there anything like an expected mankind saviour. Islâm, is as discovered by the Austrian Jewish revert to Islâm, Muhammad Asad who quoted the Qur'ân as,

$$﴿وَأَن لَّيْسَ لِلإِنسَنِ إِلَّا مَا سَعَى﴾$$

'Man can have nothing but what he does (good or bad).'[1]

"I could not find it anywhere in the Qur'ân any mention of man's need for salvation. In Islâm, there is no concept of the first inherited sin that stand between man and his fate, because Islâm does not require from man to present a sacrifice or kill himself in order to have the door of repentance opened for him and to be saved from sins."[2]

Allâh says,

$$﴿أَلَّا نَزِرُ وَازِرَةٌ وِزْرَ أُخْرَى﴾$$

"No burdened person (with sins) shall bear the burden (sins) of another."[3]

Repentance has great benefits and impacts, some of which are:

1. It makes man know expansiveness of Allâh's forbearance, and magnanimity in concealing his misdeeds. Had He willed, He would have hastened to punish him and disgraced him in front of people

---

[1] An-Najm 53:39.
[2] *Road to Islâm* by Muhammad Asad p. 140.
[3] An-Najm 53:38

so that he would not be able to live comfortably with them. But Allâh honoured him by concealing for him his sins, covered him by His forbearance and endowed him with energy, provision and sustenance.

2. It lets him know his real self, that it is inclined to evil and that whatever comes from it of sins, misdeeds or negligence is an indication from forbidden desires, and that, it cannot dispense of Allâh - for even a twinkle of an eye - for its purification and guidance.

3. Allâh prescribes repentance in order to seek with it the greatest causes of happiness for man, which is creating refuge with Allâh and seeking His assistance; and also to bring about different kinds of supplication; showing one's submission, helplessness to Allâh, showing one's love to Allâh, one's fear of and hope in Him; then the soul moves closer to its Creator in a special way which will not occur to it without repentance and escaping to Allâh.

4. It makes Allâh forgive him his past sins. Allâh says,

﴿قُل لِّلَّذِينَ كَفَرُوٓاْ إِن يَنتَهُواْ يُغْفَرْ لَهُم مَّا قَدْ سَلَفَ﴾

"Say (O Muhammad ﷺ) to those who have disbelieved, if they cease (from disbelief) their past will be forgiven."[1]

5. It makes one's evil deeds turned to good ones. Allâh says,

---

[1] Al-Anfâl 8:38.

﴿إِلَّا مَن تَابَ وَءَامَنَ وَعَمِلَ عَمَلًا صَلِحًا فَأُوْلَٰئِكَ يُبَدِّلُ ٱللَّهُ
سَيِّئَاتِهِمْ حَسَنَٰتٍ وَكَانَ ٱللَّهُ غَفُورًا رَّحِيمًا﴾

"Except those who repent and believe and do righteous deeds; for those, Allâh will change their sins into good deeds, and Allâh is Oft-forgiving, Most-Merciful." [1]

6. It enables him treat his fellow human beings when they do evil to him as he will love Allâh to treat him as regards his own misdeeds and sins; for recompense is in accordance with the type of deed. So, if he treats people in this good manner, he will also be treated by Allâh in the like manner and Allâh will be kind to him regardless of his evil deeds and sins, just as he does with his fellow human beings.

7. It enables him to know that he is full of faults and defects; this will make him refrain from speaking about the faults of other people and will be preoccupied with reforming his own self instead of thinking about the faults of others. [2]

I would like to conclude this section with the story of a man who came to the Prophet ﷺ and said,

«يَارَسُولَ الله! مَا تَرَكْتُ حَاجَةً وَلَا دَاجَةً وَلَا دَاجَةً إِلَّا قَدْ
أَتَيْتُ قَالَ : أَلَيْسَ تَشْهَدُ أَنْ لَا إِلَه إلا اللهُ، وَأَنَّ محمدًا
رسُولُ اللهِ(ثلاث مرّات قال: نَعَمْ. قَالَ: «ذَاكَ يَأْتِي عَلَى
ذَلِكَ»

"O Messenger of Allâh! I have not left any small or

---

[1] Al-Furqân 25:70.
[2] *Muftaahu daaris-sa'aadah*, Vol. 1, p. 358-370.

*big sin but I had committed it." The Messenger of
Allâh said, "Don't you testify that there is no other
deity worthy of worship except Allâh and that
Muhammad is the Messenger of Allâh?" He asked
him this question three times and the man answered
each time, "Yes." He then said, "your testimony has
erased all that (you have committed of sins)"[1]*

In another narration, the man came to the Prophet ﷺ
and said,

«أَرَأَيْتَ مَنْ عَمِلَ الذُّنُوبَ كُلَّهَا فَلَمْ يِتْرُكْ مِنْهَا شَيْئًا، وَهُوَفِي
ذَلكَ هَلْ لَهُ مِنْ توبَةٍ قَالَ : فَهَلْ أَسْلَمْتَ ؟ قَالَ: أَمَّا أَنَا
فَأَشْهَدُ أَنْ لَاإِلَهَ إِلَّا اللهُ وَحْدَهُ لَا شَرَيكَ لَهُ وَأَنَّكَ رَسُولُ اللهِ.
قَالَ: نَعَمْ تَفْعَلُ الْخَيْراتِ وَتَتْرُكَ السَّيِّئَاتِ فيَجْعَلُهُنَّ اللهُ لَكَ
خَيْرَاتٍ كُلَّهُنَّ، قَالَ: وَغُدْرَاتِي وَ فُجْراتِي؟ قَالَ : نَعَمْ، قَالَ:
اللهُ أَكْبَرُ، فَمَازَالَ يُكَبِّرُ حَتَّى تَوَارَىٰ»

*"Tell me! If a man committed all sins but has not
associated anything in worship with Allâh, and yet
did not leave any small or big sin uncommitted, can
his repentance be accepted?" The Prophet asked the
man, "have you embraced Islâm?" The man
answered, "As for me, I testify that there is no deity
worthy of worship except Allâh, that He is One and
has no partner and that you are the Messenger of
Allâh."The Prophet said, "Yes! Do good deeds and
refrain from evil ones, so that Allâh may turn all those
evil deeds to good ones for you." The man said, "Even
my acts of treachery and my sins?!"*

---

[1] Reported by Aboo Ya'laa; At-Tabaraanee; and Al-Maqdisee.

The Prophet ﷺ said, "Yes." The man said, "Allâhu Akbar (Allâh is the Most-Great) and he kept on saying that until he disappeared." [1]

Islâm therefore erases whatever sin one might have committed and sincere repentance also erases whatever sin one might have committed as authentically reported from the Prophet.

---

[1] Ibn Abee 'Aasim; At-Tabarani and Al-Bazzaar, *Majma' Az-Zawa'id*: 1/32..

The End of One Who Does Not Adhere to Islâm

As it has been made clear to you in this book that Islâm is the religion of Allâh, that it is the true religion, that it was the one preached by all Prophets and Messengers; Allâh has prepared great reward in this world and the Hereafter for whoever believes in it and threatened whoever disbelieves in it with severe torment.

Since Allâh is the Creator, the Possessor and Disposer of all this universe, and you, man, are just one of His creatures; He created you, and subjected to you all that is the universe, ordained His Law for you and commands you to obey Him. If you therefore believe, obeys His Commandment and abstain from all that He forbids you, you will attain what He promises you of the everlasting bliss in the Hereafter and you will be happy in this world with all that He will endow on you of all kinds of favours; you will then be like the wisest men and the purest of them in soul; the Prophets, Messengers, righteous people and the favoured angels.

But if you disbelieve, and disobey your Lord; you will lose your worldly life and your Hereafter and expose yourself to His wrath and punishment in this world and the Hereafter. You will then be like the most wicked of all creatures, the most defective in intelligence and the most debased in mind: the devils, corrupt people and false deities and transgressors, just to mention a few.

Let me now tell you something of the consequences of disbelief in detail:

1. *Fear and lack of security*: Allâh promises complete security in this world and the Hereafter for those who believe in Him and follow His Messengers. He says,

$$\text{﴿ ٱلَّذِينَ ءَامَنُوا۟ وَلَمْ يَلْبِسُوٓا۟ إِيمَٰنَهُم بِظُلْمٍ أُو۟لَٰٓئِكَ لَهُمُ ٱلْأَمْنُ وَهُم مُّهْتَدُونَ ﴾}$$

"Those who believe and confuse not their belief with wrong, for them there is security and they are the guided." [1]

Allâh is the Giver of security, the Watcher over His creatures, the Possessor of all that is in the universe. If He loves a slave of His because of his belief, He gives him security, tranquillity and peace, but if a slave of His disbelieves in Him, He withdraws tranquillity and security from him and you will not see such a person but afraid of his fate in the Hereafter, afraid for his own self from calamities and diseases and afraid for his future in this world. That is why the insurance market insures lives and properties for lack of security and lack of having trust in Allâh.

2. *Difficult life*: Allâh created man, subjected to him all that is in the universe and portion out for every creature his share of sustenance and lifespan. Hence you see the bird going out of its nest to

---

[1] Al-An'âm 6:82.

look for its provision and then picks it. It moves from a branch of the tree to another and sings in most melodious tone. Man is also one of these creatures for whom Allâh has portioned out his provision and lifespan. If he therefore believes in his Lord and stands firm on His Law, Allâh will give him happiness and stability and He will make his matters easy for him, even if he does not possess more than the least means of livelihood.

If he however disbelieves in his Lord and feels too big to worship Him, He will make his life straitened and make him suffer from sorrow and distress even if he has all means of comfort and enjoyment at his disposal. Don't you see the great numbers of suicide victims in countries in which all means of affluence are guaranteed for their citizens? Don't you see all kinds of furniture and mats used for the enjoyment of this life? The cause of all this extravagance is the vacuity of the heart from faith, feeling of constraint and hardship and an attempt to dismiss all these worries with all different means. Allâh says the truth in His Word,

$$﴿وَمَنْ أَعْرَضَ عَن ذِكْرِى فَإِنَّ لَهُ مَعِيشَةً ضَنكًا وَنَحْشُرُهُ يَوْمَ ٱلْقِيَـٰمَةِ أَعْمَىٰ﴾$$

"But whoever turns away from My Reminder, verily, for him is a life of hardship and We shall raise him up blind on the Day of Resurrection."[1]

3. *He will live in continuous war with his own soul and with the world around him.*

---

[1] Tâ-Hâ 20:124.

This is because, his soul is created upon Islâmic Monotheism. Allâh says,

﴾فِطْرَتَ ٱللَّهِ ٱلَّتِى فَطَرَ ٱلنَّاسَ عَلَيْهَا﴿

"Such is the way of Allâh upon which He created mankind."

His body surrenders to its Lord and moves according to His order, but the disbeliever insists on going against his own nature, and lives his voluntary life in rebellion against his Lord. Although his body surrenders to the will of the Creator, his own voluntary will is in opposition.

He will be in constant war with the world around him in the sense that, all this universe right from its greatest galaxy to its smallest insect, moves according to the way which Allâh has ordained for it. Allâh says,

﴾ثُمَّ ٱسْتَوَىٰ إِلَى ٱلسَّمَاءِ وَهِىَ دُخَانٌ فَقَالَ لَهَا وَلِلْأَرْضِ ٱئْتِيَا طَوْعًا أَوْ كَرْهًا قَالَتَآ أَتَيْنَا طَآئِعِينَ﴿

"Then He (Allâh) rose over towards the heaven when it was smoke and said to it and to the earth: 'Come both of you willingly or unwillingly,' They both said: 'We come willingly.' "[1]

The universe loves him who agrees with it in submission to Allâh and hates him who opposes it. The disbeliever is the recalcitrant in this universe for he makes himself an opponent to his Lord and contender with Him, that is why it is appropriate

---

[1] Fussilat 41:11.

for the heavens and the earth and all other creatures to hate him and his disbelief and atheism. Allâh says,

$$﴿وَقَالُوا اتَّخَذَ الرَّحْمَٰنُ وَلَدًا ۝ لَقَدْ جِئْتُمْ شَيْئًا إِدًّا ۝ تَكَادُ السَّمَوَاتُ يَتَفَطَّرْنَ مِنْهُ وَتَنشَقُّ الْأَرْضُ وَتَخِرُّ الْجِبَالُ هَدًّا ۝ أَن دَعَوْا لِلرَّحْمَٰنِ وَلَدًا ۝ وَمَا يَنبَغِي لِلرَّحْمَٰنِ أَن يَتَّخِذَ وَلَدًا ۝ إِن كُلُّ مَن فِي السَّمَوَاتِ وَالْأَرْضِ إِلَّا آتِي الرَّحْمَٰنِ عَبْدًا﴾$$

"And they say: 'The Most Gracious (Allâh) has begotten a son.' Indeed, you have brought forth (said) the terrible thing, whereby the heavens are almost torn, and the earth is split asunder, and the mountains fall in ruins, that they ascribe a son to the Most-Gracious. But it is not suitable for (the majesty) of the Most-Gracious that He should beget a son. There is none in the heavens and the earth but comes unto Most Gracious as a slave."[1]

He says about Pharaoh and his hosts,

$$﴿فَمَا بَكَتْ عَلَيْهِمُ السَّمَاءُ وَالْأَرْضُ وَمَا كَانُوا مُنظَرِينَ﴾$$

"And the heavens and the earth wept not for them, nor were they given a respite."[2]

4. *Living a life of ignorance*: For disbelief is ignorance, rather the greatest ignorance; because the disbeliever is ignorant of his Lord. He sees this universe that was created by his Lord in the most wonderful way, he sees in himself the greatness of Allâh's deed and yet he is ignorant of the Creator of this

---

[1] Maryam 19:88-93.
[2] Ad-Dukhaan 44:29.

universe and the Constructor of his own self; is this not the greatest ignorance?

5. *Living a life of one who wrongs himself and all that is around him :*

This is because, he subjected his own self for purposes other than that for which he was created. He does not worship his Lord but worship others. Injustice is to put a thing in a place to which it does not belong; and which type of injustice is greater than directing acts of worship to those who do not deserve them. Luqmaan has told his son while explaining the awfulness of polytheism,

$$﴿وَإِذْ قَالَ لُقْمَٰنُ لِٱبْنِهِۦ وَهُوَ يَعِظُهُۥ يَٰبُنَىَّ لَا تُشْرِكْ بِٱللَّهِ إِنَّ ٱلشِّرْكَ لَظُلْمٌ عَظِيمٌ﴾$$

"O my son! Join not in worship others with Allâh. Verily, joining others in worship with Allâh is a great wrong indeed."[1]

It is also injustice for the people and other creatures around him; because he does not acknowledge the right of Him to Whom right is due. On the Day of Resurrection, every man or animal he has wronged will stand before him asking Allâh to avenge for him.

6. *He exposes himself to the wrath of Allâh :*

He exposes himself to the calamities and afflictions as immediate punishment for his disbelief. Allâh says,

---
[1] Luqmân 31:13.

﴿أَفَأَمِنَ ٱلَّذِينَ مَكَرُواْ ٱلسَّيِّئَاتِ أَن يَخْسِفَ ٱللَّهُ بِهِمُ ٱلْأَرْضَ أَوْ يَأْتِيَهُمُ ٱلْعَذَابُ مِنْ حَيْثُ لَا يَشْعُرُونَ ○ أَوْ يَأْخُذَهُمْ فِى تَقَلُّبِهِمْ فَمَا هُم بِمُعْجِزِينَ ○ أَوْ يَأْخُذَهُمْ عَلَىٰ تَخَوُّفٍ فَإِنَّ رَبَّكُمْ لَرَءُوفٌ رَّحِيمٌ ○﴾

"Do then those who devise evil plots feel secure that Allâh will not sink them into the earth, or that the torment will not seize them from directions they perceive not? Or that He may catch them in the midst of their going to and from (in their jobs) so that there be no escape for them (from Allâh's punishment)? Or that He may catch them through gradual diminishing (of the wealth and health). Truly, your Lord is indeed Full of Kindness, Most-Merciful."[1]

He also says,

﴿وَلَا يَزَالُ ٱلَّذِينَ كَفَرُواْ تُصِيبُهُم بِمَا صَنَعُواْ قَارِعَةٌ أَوْ تَحُلُّ قَرِيبًا مِّن دَارِهِمْ حَتَّىٰ يَأْتِىَ وَعْدُ ٱللَّهِ إِنَّ ٱللَّهَ لَا يُخْلِفُ ٱلْمِيعَادَ﴾

"And a disaster will not cease to strike those who disbelieved because of their (evil)deeds or it settles close their homes, until the Promise of Allâh comes to pass. Certainly, Allâh breaks not His Promise."[2]

He says in another verse,

﴿أَوَ أَمِنَ أَهْلُ ٱلْقُرَىٰ أَن يَأْتِيَهُم بَأْسُنَا ضُحًى وَهُمْ يَلْعَبُونَ﴾

"Or did the people of the towns then feel secure against the coming of Our punishment in the forenoon while they were playing?"[3]

---

[1] An-Nahl 16:45-47.
[2] Ar-Ra'd 13:31.
[3] Al-A'râf 7:98.

This is the fate of every man who turns away from Remembrance of Allâh. Allâh tells us of the punishments of past nations who were disbelievers,

﴿فَكُلًّا أَخَذْنَا بِذَنبِهِۦ فَمِنْهُم مَّنْ أَرْسَلْنَا عَلَيْهِ حَاصِبًا وَمِنْهُم مَّنْ أَخَذَتْهُ ٱلصَّيْحَةُ وَمِنْهُم مَّنْ خَسَفْنَا بِهِ ٱلْأَرْضَ وَمِنْهُم مَّنْ أَغْرَقْنَا وَمَا كَانَ ٱللَّهُ لِيَظْلِمَهُمْ وَلَٰكِن كَانُوٓا۟ أَنفُسَهُمْ يَظْلِمُونَ﴾

"So We punished each (of them) for his sins; of them are some of whom We sent a violent wind, and of them were those who were overtaken by torment - awful cry, and of them were some of whom We caused the earth to swallow and of them were some whom We drowned. It was not Allâh Who wronged them, but they wronged themselves."[1]

7. *Failure and loss will be his lot:* Because of his wrong, he looses the greatest thing with which the hearts and souls enjoy, which is knowing Allâh, meditating in Him and feeling tranquillity with Him. He also looses the world, for he lives there a wretched and confused life and he looses his own soul for which he amasses the wealth of this world; for he subjects it for a purpose different from that which it was created for. He thereby does not attain with it happiness in this world, for he makes it lived in misery and caused it to die in misery and it shall be raised up among the miserable. Allâh says,

﴿وَمَنْ خَفَّتْ مَوَٰزِينُهُ فَأُو۟لَٰٓئِكَ ٱلَّذِينَ خَسِرُوٓا۟ أَنفُسَهُمْ﴾

---

[1] Al-Ankabût 29:40.

"As for those whose scale will be light, they are those who will loose their own selves."[1]

He will also loose his family, for he lived with them on disbelief in Allâh and they will also be like him in misery and hardship and their fate will be Fire. Allâh says,

﴿إِنَّ ٱلۡخَٰسِرِينَ ٱلَّذِينَ خَسِرُوٓاْ أَنفُسَهُمۡ وَأَهۡلِيهِمۡ يَوۡمَ ٱلۡقِيَٰمَةِ﴾

"The losers are those will loose themselves and their families on the Day of Resurrection."[2]

On the Day of Resurrection, they will be led to Fire, and evil is it as a resting place. Allâh says,

﴿ٱحۡشُرُواْ ٱلَّذِينَ ظَلَمُواْ وَأَزۡوَٰجَهُمۡ وَمَا كَانُواْ يَعۡبُدُونَ ٠ مِن دُونِ ٱللَّهِ فَٱهۡدُوهُمۡ إِلَىٰ صِرَٰطِ ٱلۡجَحِيمِ﴾

"(It will be said to the angels): 'Assemble those who did wrong, together with their spouses and what they used to worship instead of Allâh and lead them on to the way of Flaming Fire.'"[3]

8. He will live as a disbeliever in his Lord and a denier of His blessings: For Allâh created him from nothing and showered on him favours, how can he then worship, befriend and thank others besides Him? Which ingratitude is greater and more heinous than this?

9. He will be denied real and purposeful life: This is because the man who deserves life is the one who

---

[1] Al-A'râf 7:9.

[2] Az-Zumar 39:15, Shooraa 42:45.

[3] As-Sâffât 37:22-23.

believes in his Lord, knows his goal, recognizes his
fate and is certain of his resurrection. He thereby
gives right to whom it is due. He does not suppress
truth nor harm a creature. He then lives the life of
happy people and attains good life in this world
and the Hereafter. Allâh says,

﴿مَنْ عَمِلَ صَلِحًا مِّن ذَكَرٍ أَوْ أُنثَىٰ وَهُوَ مُؤْمِنٌ فَلَنُحْيِيَنَّهُ حَيَوٰةً
طَيِّبَةً﴾

*"Whoever works righteousness - whether male or
female while he (or she) is a true believer, verily, to
him (or her) We will give a good life."* [1]

And in the Hereafter, his reward will be,

﴿وَمَسَٰكِنَ طَيِّبَةً فِى جَنَّٰتِ عَدْنٍ ذَٰلِكَ ٱلْفَوْزُ ٱلْعَظِيمُ﴾

*"Pleasant dwellings in (Eden) Paradise; that is
indeed, the great success."* [2]

But whoever lives in this world like animals, such
does not know his Lord or his goal and fate his only
aim is to eat, drink and sleep. What then is the
difference between him and other animals? He is
even in greater error than animals. Allâh says,

﴿وَلَقَدْ ذَرَأْنَا لِجَهَنَّمَ كَثِيرًا مِّنَ ٱلْجِنِّ وَٱلْإِنسِ لَهُمْ قُلُوبٌ لَّا يَفْقَهُونَ
بِهَا وَلَهُمْ أَعْيُنٌ لَّا يُبْصِرُونَ بِهَا وَلَهُمْ ءَاذَانٌ لَّا يَسْمَعُونَ بِهَا أُوْلَٰٓئِكَ كَٱلْأَنْعَٰمِ
بَلْ هُمْ أَضَلُّ أُوْلَٰٓئِكَ هُمُ ٱلْغَٰفِلُونَ﴾

*"And surely, We have created many of the jinn and
mankind for Hell. They have hearts wherewith they*

---
[1] An-Nahl 16:97.
[2] As-Saff 61:12.

*understand not, and they have eyes wherewith they
see not, and they have ears wherewith they hear not
(the truth). They are like cattle, nay even more astray;
Those! They are the heedless ones."* [1]

He also says,

﴿أَمْ تَحْسَبُ أَنَّ أَكْثَرَهُمْ يَسْمَعُونَ أَوْ يَعْقِلُونَ إِنْ هُمْ إِلَّا كَٱلْأَنْعَمِ
بَلْ هُمْ أَضَلُّ سَبِيلًا﴾

*"Or do you think that most of them hear or
understand? They are only like cattle - nay, they are
even further astray from the path."* [2]

10. **He abides forever in the torment:** This is because
the disbeliever moves from a torment to another.
He goes out of this world - after he has tasted all its
agonies and afflictions - to the Hereafter. In the first
stage of the Hereafter, the angels of death come
upon him and before them come the angels of
torment who will give him his deserved punishment. Allâh says,

﴿وَلَوْ تَرَىٰ إِذْ يَتَوَفَّى ٱلَّذِينَ كَفَرُواْ ٱلْمَلَٰٓئِكَةُ يَضْرِبُونَ وُجُوهَهُمْ
وَأَدْبَٰرَهُمْ﴾

*"And if you could see when the angels take away the
souls of those who disbelieve (at death); they smite
their faces and their backs."* [3]

Then his soul departs and when he is put in the grave,
he meets a greater torment. Allâh says about the

---

[1] Al-A'râf 7:179.
[2] Al-Furqân 25:44.
[3] Al-Anfâl 8:50.

People of Pharaoh,

$$﴿ٱلنَّارُ يُعْرَضُونَ عَلَيْهَا غُدُوًّا وَعَشِيًّا وَيَوْمَ تَقُومُ ٱلسَّاعَةُ أَدْخِلُوٓا۟ ءَالَ فِرْعَوْنَ أَشَدَّ ٱلْعَذَابِ ﴾$$

"They are exposed to Fire, morning and afternoon and on the Day when the Hour will be established, (it will be said to the angels): 'Make Pharaoh people enter the severest torment' "[1]

On the Day of Resurrection, when the creatures are raised up and the deeds are exposed and the disbeliever sees that Allâh has accurately enumerated all his deeds in that book about which He says,

$$﴿ وَوُضِعَ ٱلْكِتَبُ فَتَرَى ٱلْمُجْرِمِينَ مُشْفِقِينَ مِمَّا فِيهِ وَيَقُولُونَ يَوَيْلَتَنَا مَالِ هَذَا ٱلْكِتَبِ لَا يُغَادِرُ صَغِيرَةً وَلَا كَبِيرَةً إِلَّآ أَحْصَنَهَاۚ ﴾$$

"And the book of record will be placed and you will see the sinners (disbelievers) fearful of that which is (recorded) therein. They will say: 'Woe to us! What sort of book is this that leaves neither small thing nor a big thing but has recorded it with numbers!' "[2]

Here, the disbeliever will wish to be dust. Allâh says,

$$﴿ إِنَّآ أَنذَرْنَكُمْ عَذَابًا قَرِيبًا يَوْمَ يَنظُرُ ٱلْمَرْءُ مَا قَدَّمَتْ يَدَاهُ وَيَقُولُ ٱلْكَافِرُ يَلَيْتَنِى كُنتُ تُرَٰبَۢا ﴾$$

"The Day when man will see that (the deeds) which his hands have sent forth, and the disbeliever will say:

---

[1] Ghâfir 40:46.
[2] Al-Ka'hf 18:49.

'Woe to me! Would that I were dust.' "[1]

Because of the horror of that Day, man will wish that he owns all that is in the earth, so that he can ransom himself with it from the torment of that Day.

﴿وَلَوْ أَنَّ لِلَّذِينَ ظَلَمُوا۟ مَا فِى ٱلْأَرْضِ جَمِيعًا وَمِثْلَهُۥ مَعَهُۥ لَٱفْتَدَوْا۟ بِهِۦ مِن سُوٓءِ ٱلْعَذَابِ يَوْمَ ٱلْقِيَـٰمَةِ﴾

"And those who did wrong; if they had all that is in the earth and therewith as much again, they verily would offer it to ransom themselves therewith on the Day of Resurrection from the evil torment." [2]

Allâh also says,

﴿يُبَصَّرُونَهُمْ يَوَدُّ ٱلْمُجْرِمُ لَوْ يَفْتَدِى مِنْ عَذَابِ يَوْمِئِذٍ بِبَنِيهِ ٠ وَصَـٰحِبَتِهِۦ وَأَخِيهِ ٠ وَفَصِيلَتِهِ ٱلَّتِى تُـْٔوِيهِ ٠ وَمَن فِى ٱلْأَرْضِ جَمِيعًا ثُمَّ يُنجِيهِ﴾

"The sinner would desire to ransom himself from the punishment of that Day by his children; and his wife and his brother and his kindred who sheltered him, and all that are in the earth, so that it might save him." [3]

For, that abode is that of recompense and not of wishful thinking. Man must therefore, get a reward for his deed; if it is good he gets good reward and if it is evil, he gets rewarded with punishment. And the worst punishment that a disbeliever may meet on the Day of Resurrection is that of Fire in which Allâh has provided different kinds of retribution for its dwellers

---

[1] An-Naba' 78:40.
[2] Az-Zumar 39:47.
[3] Al-Ma'ârij 70:11-14.

so that they can taste the torment of their deeds. Allâh says,

$$﴿هَٰذِهِۦ جَهَنَّمُ ٱلَّتِى يُكَذِّبُ بِهَا ٱلْمُجْرِمُونَ ۝ يَطُوفُونَ بَيْنَهَا وَبَيْنَ حَمِيمٍ ءَانٍ﴾$$

"This is the Hell which the sinners (disbelievers) denied. They will go between it and the fierce boiling water."[1]

He also informs us of the garments of the dwellers of Hell,

$$﴿فَٱلَّذِينَ كَفَرُواْ قُطِّعَتْ لَهُمْ ثِيَابٌ مِّن نَّارٍ يُصَبُّ مِن فَوْقِ رُءُوسِهِمُ ٱلْحَمِيمُ ۝ يُصْهَرُ بِهِۦ مَا فِى بُطُونِهِمْ وَٱلْجُلُودُ ۝ وَلَهُم مَّقَٰمِعُ مِنْ حَدِيدٍ﴾$$

"As for those who disbelieved, garments of fire will be cut out for them, boiling water will be poured down over their heads. With it will melt (or vanish away) what is within their bellies as well as their skins; and for them are hooked rods of iron."[2]

---

[1] Ar-Rahmân 55:43-44.

[2] Al-Hajj 22:19-21.

The End

O man! You were before a non-existent. Allâh says,

﴿أَوَلَا يَذْكُرُ ٱلْإِنسَٰنُ أَنَّا خَلَقْنَٰهُ مِن قَبْلُ وَلَمْ يَكُ شَيْئًا﴾

"Does not man remember that We created him before while he was nothing?"[1]

Then He created you from a mixture of male and female discharge and made you hearing, seeing. Allâh says,

﴿هَلْ أَتَىٰ عَلَى ٱلْإِنسَٰنِ حِينٌ مِّنَ ٱلدَّهْرِ لَمْ يَكُن شَيْئًا مَّذْكُورًا ۝ إِنَّا خَلَقْنَا ٱلْإِنسَٰنَ مِن نُّطْفَةٍ أَمْشَاجٍ نَّبْتَلِيهِ فَجَعَلْنَٰهُ سَمِيعًا بَصِيرًا ۝﴾

"Has there not been over man a period of time, when he was not a thing worth mentioning? Verily, We have created man from drop of mixed sexual discharge of man and woman in order to try him; so We made him hearer and seer."[2]

Then you moved gradually from a state of weakness to strength and you shall be returned to a state of weakness again. Allâh says,

﴿ٱللَّهُ ٱلَّذِى خَلَقَكُم مِّن ضَعْفٍ ثُمَّ جَعَلَ مِنۢ بَعْدِ ضَعْفٍ قُوَّةً ثُمَّ جَعَلَ مِنۢ بَعْدِ قُوَّةٍ ضَعْفًا وَشَيْبَةً يَخْلُقُ مَا يَشَآءُ وَهُوَ ٱلْعَلِيمُ ٱلْقَدِيرُ﴾

"Allâh is He Who created you, in (a state of)

---

[1] Maryam 19:67.
[2] Al-Insân 76:1-2.

weakness, then gave you strength after weakness, then
after strength gave (you) weakness and grey hair. He
creates what He wills and it is He Who is the All-
Knowing, the All-Powerful" [1]

Then the end is death and you, through these stages,
move from weakness to weakness; you cannot avert
evil from yourself nor can you bring about benefit for
yourself except by using that strength and provision
that Allâh gave you. You are by nature poor and
needy. Many are the things that you need to remain
alive which you do not possess or which you
sometimes have and sometime are deprived of.
Many are also those things that are useful to you
and you would like to have and which you achieve
sometimes and do not achieve other times. Many are
things that harm you, ditch your hope, waste your
efforts and bring on you tribulations and calamity
which you would like to avert; and which you
sometimes succeed in averting and which you fail
sometimes to avert. In view of this, do you not feel
your helplessness and your need to Allâh? Allâh says,

يَٰٓأَيُّهَا ٱلنَّاسُ أَنتُمُ ٱلۡفُقَرَآءُ إِلَى ٱللَّهِ وَٱللَّهُ هُوَ ٱلۡغَنِيُّ ٱلۡحَمِيدُ ۝

"O you people! It is you who stand in need of Allâh.
But Allâh is Rich (free of all needs) Worthy of all
praise." [2]

You are exposed to a weak virus which you cannot see
with your naked eyes, and that causes you painful
disease which you cannot prevent and you then go to

---

[1] Ar-Rûm 30:54.
[2] Fâtir 35:15.

a weak human being like yourself to treat you.
Sometimes, the medicine works and sometimes the
doctor fails to cure you and both you and your doctor
then become confused.

O man! What a weak creature you are when the fly
snatches something from you and you cannot take
back from it! Allâh says the truth when He says,

﴿يَٰٓأَيُّهَا ٱلنَّاسُ ضُرِبَ مَثَلٌ فَٱسْتَمِعُوا۟ لَهُۥٓ إِنَّ ٱلَّذِينَ تَدْعُونَ
مِن دُونِ ٱللَّهِ لَن يَخْلُقُوا۟ ذُبَابًا وَلَوِ ٱجْتَمَعُوا۟ لَهُۥ وَإِن يَسْلُبْهُمُ ٱلذُّبَابُ
شَيْـًٔا لَّا يَسْتَنقِذُوهُ مِنْهُ ضَعُفَ ٱلطَّالِبُ وَٱلْمَطْلُوبُ﴾

*"O mankind! A similitude has been coined, so listen to
it: Verily, those on whom you call besides Allâh
cannot create (even) a fly, even though they combine
together for the purpose. And if the fly snatches away
a thing from them, they will have no power to release
it from the fly. So weak are (both) the seeker and the
sought."* [1]

If you cannot take back what the fly snatches away
from you, which then of your affairs do you have
control over? Your forelock is in the hand of Allâh, so
is your soul. Our heart is between two of His fingers
which He turns round as He wills. Your life, death,
happiness and misery are all in His Hand.

Your undertakings and sayings are by the permission
of Allâh and His Will. You do not move except with
His permission and you do not perform any act except
by His Will. If He leaves you to yourself, He leaves
you to weakness, negligence, sin and misdeed; and if

---

[1] Al-Hajj 22:73.

He leaves you for others, He leaves you with the one who cannot avail you of any benefit, harm, death, life or resurrection. You cannot dispense of Allâh for a twinkle of an eye. You rather need Him in every aspect as long as you live. You invite His wrath with sins and disbelief though you seriously need Him in all aspects. You forgot Him though, your return is to Him and it is in front of Him that you shall stand.[1]

O man! As a result of your weakness and your inability to shoulder the consequences of your sins that

﴿يُرِيدُ ٱللَّهُ أَن يُخَفِّفَ عَنكُمْ وَخُلِقَ ٱلْإِنسَٰنُ ضَعِيفًا﴾

"Allâh wishes to lighten (the burden) for you and man was created weak."[2]

He sent Messengers, revealed Books, ordained Laws, established the Straight Path before you and established signs, proofs and evidences and made in everything a sign that shows His Oneness, Lordship and His sole right to be worshipped. But in spite of all this, you block the truth with falsehood, take Satan as a friend besides Allâh and argue with falsehood.

﴿وَلَقَدْ صَرَّفْنَا فِى هَٰذَا ٱلْقُرْءَانِ لِلنَّاسِ مِن كُلِّ مَثَلٍ وَكَانَ ٱلْإِنسَٰنُ أَكْثَرَ شَىْءٍ جَدَلًا﴾

"Man is ever more quarrelsome than anything"[3]

Allâh's favours in which you move and enjoy have made you forget your beginning and end! Don't you

---

[1] From *Al-Fawaaid* by Ibn Al-Qayyim.
[2] An-Nisâ' 4:28.
[3] Al-Kahf 18:54.

remember that you were created from a mixed sexual discharge, that your return will be to a grave and that final destination after Resurrection will either be Paradise or Fire? Allâh says,

﴿أَوَلَمْ يَرَ ٱلْإِنسَـٰنُ أَنَّا خَلَقْنَـٰهُ مِن نُّطْفَةٍ فَإِذَا هُوَ خَصِيمٌ مُّبِينٌ ٠ وَضَرَبَ لَنَا مَثَلًا وَنَسِىَ خَلْقَهُۥ قَالَ مَن يُحْىِ ٱلْعِظَـٰمَ وَهِىَ رَمِيمٌ ٠ قُلْ يُحْيِيهَا ٱلَّذِىٓ أَنشَأَهَآ أَوَّلَ مَرَّةٍ وَهُوَ بِكُلِّ خَلْقٍ عَلِيمٌ﴾

"Does not man see that We have created him from a mixed drop of sexual discharge, yet behold, he (stands forth) as an open opponent, and he puts for Us forth a parable and forgets his own creation. He says: 'Who will give life to the bones after they are rotten and have become dust?' Say (O Muhammad ﷺ*): He will give life to them Who Created them for the first time! And He is the All-Knower of every creation!"* [1]

He also says,

﴿يَـٰٓأَيُّهَا ٱلْإِنسَـٰنُ مَا غَرَّكَ بِرَبِّكَ ٱلْكَرِيمِ ٠ ٱلَّذِى خَلَقَكَ فَسَوَّىٰكَ فَعَدَلَكَ ٠ فِىٓ أَىِّ صُورَةٍ مَّا شَآءَ رَكَّبَكَ﴾

"O man what has made you careless about your Lord, the Most-Generous? Who created you, fashioned you perfectly and gave you due proportion. In whatever form he willed, He put you together." [2]

O man! Why are you denying yourself the joy of standing before your Lord, meditating with Him, so that He can enrich you out of poverty, heal you from your ailment, relieve you of your sorrow, forgive your

---

[1] Yâ-Sîn 36:77-79.
[2] Al-Infitâr 82:6-8

sins, remove your harm, help you when you are
wronged, guide you when you are confused or go
astray, give you knowledge when you are ignorant,
give you security when you are frightened, show
mercy to you when you are weak, drive away your
enemies and provide for you your livelihood.[1]

O man! The greatest blessing that Allâh endowed man
with after that of the religion is the blessing of
intelligence, so that he can distinguish with it
between what benefits him and what harms him, to
understand the commandments and prohibitions of
Allâh and in order to know by it, the greatest goal
which is to worship Allâh alone Who has no partner.
Allâh says,

$$﴿وَمَا بِكُم مِّن نِّعْمَةٍ فَمِنَ ٱللَّهِ ثُمَّ إِذَا مَسَّكُمُ ٱلضُّرُّ فَإِلَيْهِ تَجْـَٔرُونَ
○ ثُمَّ إِذَا كَشَفَ ٱلضُّرَّ عَنكُمْ إِذَا فَرِيقٌ مِّنكُم بِرَبِّهِمْ يُشْرِكُونَ﴾$$

*"And whatever of blessings and good things you have,
it is from Allâh, and when harm touches you unto
Him you cry aloud for help. Then when He has
removed the harm from you, behold, some of you
associate others in worship with their Lord."*[2]

O you man! The wise person loves lofty matters and
abhors debased ones. He loves to emulate every
righteous and magnanimous among the Prophets
and pious people and yearns to join them even if he
cannot reach their status. The only way to that is what
Allâh directs us to when He says,

---

[1] *Miftaah daaris-sa'aadah* 1, p. 251.
[2] An-Nahl 16:53-54.

$$﴿قُلْ إِن كُنتُمْ تُحِبُّونَ ٱللَّهَ فَٱتَّبِعُونِي يُحْبِبْكُمُ ٱللَّهُ وَيَغْفِرْ لَكُمْ ذُنُوبَكُمْ وَٱللَّهُ غَفُورٌ رَّحِيمٌ﴾$$

"If you (really) love Allâh, then follow me (Muhammad ﷺ) Allâh will love you and forgive you your sins."[1]

If man can do this, Allâh will make him join the rank of the Prophets, the Messengers, the Martyrs and righteous people. Allâh says,

$$﴿وَمَن يُطِعِ ٱللَّهَ وَٱلرَّسُولَ فَأُوْلَٰٓئِكَ مَعَ ٱلَّذِينَ أَنْعَمَ ٱللَّهُ عَلَيْهِم مِّنَ ٱلنَّبِيِّـۧنَ وَٱلصِّدِّيقِينَ وَٱلشُّهَدَآءِ وَٱلصَّٰلِحِينَ وَحَسُنَ أُوْلَٰٓئِكَ رَفِيقًا﴾$$

"And whosoever obeys Allâh and the Messenger (Muhammad ﷺ), then they will be in the company of those on whom Allâh has bestowed His Grace of the Prophets, the Siddiqqeen, the Martyrs and the righteous. And how excellent these companions are!"[2]

O you man! I advise you that you go into a seclusion with yourself and think deeply of the truth that has come to you reflect over the proofs and evidences; if you find it to be truth hasten to follow it and do not be a slave of customs and traditions. Know that your own soul is dearer to you than your friends, companions and heritage of your fore-fathers. Allâh has admonished the disbelievers with this and called them to it. He says,

$$﴿قُلْ إِنَّمَآ أَعِظُكُم بِوَٰحِدَةٍ أَن تَقُومُوا۟ لِلَّهِ مَثْنَىٰ وَفُرَٰدَىٰ ثُمَّ$$

---
[1] Aal 'Imrân 3:31.
[2] An-Nisâ' 4:69.

$$﴿تَفَكَّرُوا۟ مَا بِصَاحِبِكُم مِّن جِنَّةٍ إِنْ هُوَ إِلَّا نَذِيرٌ لَّكُم بَيْنَ يَدَىْ عَذَابٍ شَدِيدٍ﴾$$

*"I exhort you to one (thing) only; that you stand up
for Allâh's sake in pairs and singly and reflect. There
is no madness in your companion (Muhammad ﷺ).
He is only a warner to you in face of a severe
torment."* [1]

O man! When you accept Islâm, you stand to lose
nothing. Allâh says,

$$﴿وَمَاذَا عَلَيْهِمْ لَوْ ءَامَنُوا۟ بِٱللَّهِ وَٱلْيَوْمِ ٱلْءَاخِرِ وَأَنفَقُوا۟ مِمَّا رَزَقَهُمُ ٱللَّهُ وَكَانَ ٱللَّهُ بِهِمْ عَلِيمًا﴾$$

*"And what loss have they if they had believed in Allâh
and the Last Day and they spend out of what Allâh
has given them for sustenance? And Allâh is Ever
All-Knower of them."* [2]

Ibn Katheer said, "What would have harmed them had
they believed in Allâh, followed the praiseworthy
way, believed in Allâh hoping for His promise in the
Hereafter for him who did good deeds and spent out
of what He has given them in ways which He loves
and is pleased with? He knows their good and evil
intentions; he knows who deserved success among
them so that He might give him success and show him
guidance and appoint him for good deeds with which
he is pleased. He also knows who deserves disgrace
and expulsion from His Divine Affection which
whoever is expelled from the door of Allâh has

---

[1] Saba' 34:46.
[2] An-Nisâ' 4:39.

failed and lost in this world and the Hereafter."[1]

Your Islâm does not stand between you and anything
that you want to do or to have among the things that
Allâh has made lawful for you. Rather, you will be
rewarded for any good deed you do in which you seek
the pleasure of Allâh even if that is in the interest of
your worldly life or increases your wealth or portion
or fame. Even the lawful things that you use, when
you make do with only the lawful and abstain from
unlawful, you will be rewarded for that. The
Messenger ﷺ of Allâh said,

«وَفِي بُضْعِ أَحَدِكُمْ صَدَقَةٌ» قَالُوا: يَا رَسُولَ اللهِ! أَيَأْتِي أَحَدُنَا
شَهْوَتَهُ وَيَكُونُ لَهُ فِيهَا أَجْرٌ؟ قَالَ: أَرَأَيْتُمْ لَوْوَضَعَهَا فِي حَرَامٍ
أَكَانَ عَلَيْهِ فِيهَا أَجْرٌ قَالَ: أَرَأَيْتُمْ لَوْ وَضَعَهَا فِي حَرَامٍ، أَكَانَ
عَلَيْهِ فِيهَا وِزْرٌ؟ فَكَذَلِكَ إِذَا وَضَعَهَا فِي الْحَلَالِ كَانَ لَهُ أَجْرٌ»

*"There is an act of charity in satiating your sexual
desire." The companions said, "O Messenger of Allâh!
Will anyone of us satiate his desire and still get
reward for that?" He answered, "Tell me, if he satiates
it in an unlawful way, will he be committing a sin by
that? Likewise, if he satiates it in the lawful way, he
will have reward for that."[2]*

O man! The Messengers have brought the truth and
conveyed the will of Allâh, and man needs to know
the Law of Allâh so as to live his life with sure
knowledge and to be among the successful in the
Hereafter. Allâh says,

[1] See Ibn Katheer 1/497.
[2] Muslim (1006)

﴿يَـٰٓأَيُّهَا ٱلنَّاسُ قَدْ جَآءَكُمُ ٱلرَّسُولُ بِٱلْحَقِّ مِن رَّبِّكُمْ فَـَٔامِنُوا۟ خَيْرًا لَّكُمْ
وَإِن تَكْفُرُوا۟ فَإِنَّ لِلَّهِ مَا فِى ٱلسَّمَـٰوَٰتِ وَٱلْأَرْضِ وَكَانَ ٱللَّهُ عَلِيمًا حَكِيمًا﴾

*"O Mankind! Verily, there has come to you the
Messenger (Muhammad ﷺ) with the truth from your
Lord. So believe in him, it is better for you. But if you
disbelieve, then certainly to Allâh belongs all that is in
heavens and in the earth. And Allâh is Ever All-
Knowing, All-Wise."* [1]

He also says,

﴿قُلْ يَـٰٓأَيُّهَا ٱلنَّاسُ قَدْ جَآءَكُمُ ٱلْحَقُّ مِن رَّبِّكُمْ فَمَنِ ٱهْتَدَىٰ فَإِنَّمَا
يَهْتَدِى لِنَفْسِهِۦ وَمَن ضَلَّ فَإِنَّمَا يَضِلُّ عَلَيْهَا وَمَآ أَنَا۠ عَلَيْكُم بِوَكِيلٍ﴾

*"Say (O Muhammad ﷺ): O Mankind! Now truth has
come to you from your Lord. So whoever receives
guidance, he does so for the good of his own self; and
whosoever goes astray, he does so to his own loss; and
I am not (set) over you as a disposer of affairs."* [2]

O man! If you embrace Islâm, you benefit none but
yourself, and if you disbelieve you harm none but
your own self. Allâh is in no need of His slaves. Sin of
the sinners does not harm Him nor does acts of
obedience of the obedient ones benefit Him. He is not
disobeyed unless by His knowledge and He is not
obeyed except with His permission. Allâh says in what
was reported from Him by His Prophet,

«يَا عِبَادِي! إِنِّي حَرَّمْتُ الظُّلْمَ عَلَىٰ نَفْسِي، وَجَعَلْتُهُ بَيْنَكُمْ
مُحَرَّمًا، فَلَا تَظَالَمُوا، يَا عِبَادِي! كُلُّكُمْ ضَالٌّ إِلَّا مَنْ هَدَيْتُهُ،

---

[1] An-Nisâ' 4:170.
[2] Yûnus 10:108.

فَاسْتَهْدُونِي أَهْدِكُمْ، يَا عِبَادِي! كُلُّكُمْ جَائِعٌ إِلَّا مَنْ أَطْعَمْتُهُ،
فَاسْتَطْعِمُونِي أُطْعِمْكُمْ، يَا عِبَادِي! كُلُّكُمْ عَارٍ إِلَّا مَنْ كَسَوْتُهُ،
فَاسْتَكْسُونِي أَكْسُكُمْ، يَا عِبَادِي! إِنَّكُمْ تُخْطِئُونَ بِاللَّيْلِ
وَالنَّهَارِ، وَأَنَا أَغْفِرُ الذُّنُوبَ جَمِيعًا، فَاسْتَغْفِرُونِي أَغْفِرْ لَكُمْ،
يَا عِبَادِي! إِنَّكُمْ لَنْ تَبْلُغُوا ضَرِّي فَتَضُرُّونِي، وَلَنْ تَبْلُغُوا نَفْعِي
فَتَنْفَعُونِي، يَا عِبَادِي! لَوْ أَنَّ أَوَّلَكُمْ وَآخِرَكُمْ، وَإِنْسَكُمْ
وَجِنَّكُمْ، كَانُوا عَلَىٰ أَتْقَىٰ قَلْبِ رَجُلٍ وَاحِدٍ مِنْكُمْ، مَا زَادَ
ذٰلِكَ فِي مُلْكِي شَيْئًا، يَا عِبَادِي! لَوْ أَنَّ أَوَّلَكُمْ وَآخِرَكُمْ،
وَإِنْسَكُمْ وَجِنَّكُمْ، كَانُوا عَلَىٰ أَفْجَرِ قَلْبِ رَجُلٍ وَاحِدٍ مِنْكُمْ، مَا
نَقَصَ ذٰلِكَ مِنْ مُلْكِي شَيْئًا، يَا عِبَادِي! لَوْ أَنَّ أَوَّلَكُمْ وَآخِرَكُمْ،
وَإِنْسَكُمْ وَجِنَّكُمْ، قَامُوا فِي صَعِيدٍ وَاحِدٍ فَسَأَلُونِي، فَأَعْطَيْتُ
كُلَّ إِنْسَانٍ مَسْأَلَتَهُ، مَا نَقَصَ ذٰلِكَ مِمَّا عِنْدِي إِلَّا كَمَا يَنْقُصُ
الْمِخْيَطُ إِذَا أُدْخِلَ الْبَحْرَ، يَا عِبَادِي! إِنَّمَا هِيَ أَعْمَالُكُمْ
أُحْصِيهَا لَكُمْ، ثُمَّ أُوَفِّيكُمْ إِيَّاهَا، فَمَنْ وَجَدَ خَيْرًا فَلْيَحْمَدِ اللَّهَ،
وَمَنْ وَجَدَ غَيْرَ ذٰلِكَ فَلَا يَلُومَنَّ إِلَّا نَفْسَهُ»

"O My Slaves! I have made injustice forbidden for
myself and I have also made it forbidden amongst you,
so do not wrong one another. O My slaves! You are all
in error except him whom I guide so seek guidance
from Me, I will guide you. O May slaves! All of you
are hungry except whom I feed so seek food from Me, I
will feed you. O My slaves! All of you are naked
except him who I clothe; so seek clothing from Me, I
will clothe you! O My slaves! You commit sins by day
and night, but I forgive all sins. So seek forgiveness
from Me, I will forgive you. O My slaves! You can
never be able to harm Me; and you can never be able to
benefit yourselves, let alone benefiting Me. O My

slaves! If the first and the last of you, and all the jinn and mankind among you were to be as pious as the most pious one among you, that adds nothing to My Kingdom. O My slaves! If the first and the last among you, and all the jinn and mankind of you are to be as sinful as the most sinful one amongst you, that decreases nothing from My Kingdom. O My slaves! If the first of you and the last among you were to stand at one place and ask Me and I grant to each and everyone his request, that decreases nothing from My Kingdom except like what a thread reduces from the ocean when it is dipped inside it and then withdrawn. O My slaves! These are only your deeds that I enumerate accurately for you, and upon which I give you reward. So whoever finds good reward, let him thank Allâh, but whoever finds anything else, let him not blame but himself." [1]

All praise is due to Allâh, Lord of the worlds. May peace and blessings be upon the noblest of all Prophets and Messengers. Our Prophet Muhammad ﷺ, as well as his household and Companions together.

---

[1] Reported by Muslim (2577), Darussalam (6572)